What business owners and other savvy business people are saying about *Roy's Rules:*

"*Roy's Rules* is must reading for refugees from downsized corporations and anyone else thinking of moving into the rewarding but tough world of small business."
  • **F. Rigdon Currie**, Partner, MK Global Ventures, Venture Capitalists, San Francisco, California

"As a commercial banker for over twenty years, I can really appreciate *Roy's Rules*. They are exactly what a banker wants his clients to put into practice every day. I recommend *Roy's Rules* to all of my clients. Thanks . . . you have made my job a little easier."
  • **David A. Grisso**, Senior Vice President, The Empire National Bank, Clarksburg, West Virginia

"If you are more interested in building financial security than playing the growth financing game, you really need to read *Roy's Rules*. Its prescription for small company success gives business owners real control over their lives.
  • **Robert K. Anderson**, Chairman, VALLEYLAB, Boulder, Colorado

"Small to mid-range company owners simply must read *Roy's Rules*. Roy Jacobson tells you in plain English what you need to know—and to plan around—when operating a solidly successful business."
  • **Jeff Moore**, Broker/Owner, Realty Executives of Nevada, Las Vegas, Nevada

"In *Roy's Rules*, you'll find twelve hands-on secrets for making good money and enjoying a great life in small business . . . even if you're up against low-wage, global competitors."
  • **Carter Henderson**, Author of *Winners: The Successful Strategies Entrepreneurs Use to Build New Businesses,* St. Augustine, Florida

"**B**usiness owners get bombarded with too many ideas on how to succeed. *Roy's Rules* cuts through all that and helps owners focus on the truly important factors that can lead them to ultimate success."

    • **Peter E. Grogan**, Owner, Ink Kraft Inc., Printing and Graphic Services, Jacksonville, Florida

"**T**o improve my financial results and lead the balanced life I want to enjoy, I know I need to put *Roy's Rules* to work in my business and my life. I've tried it, and it works!"

    • **Dick Peterson**, Owner, Larner Machine Inc., Precision Machinists, Phoenix, Arizona

"**S**avvy, timely, pragmatic advice. *Roy's Rules* effectively capsulizes one of the critical, emerging strategies, and perhaps the soundest, for managing your own business for solid success in the new economy. Business unit managers in larger corporations would benefit from applying *Roy's Rules* as well."

    • **Harry S. Dent, Jr.**, Author, *The Great Boom Ahead*, Moss Beach, California

"**S**mall business owners have a natural advantage over the professional managers of giant corporations. They can exploit that advantage and achieve a balanced life by living *Roy's Rules.*"

    • **Craig R. Hickman**, Best-Selling Author of *The Strategy Game* and *Creating Excellence*, Provo, Utah

"**G**reat book. I wish Roy were on my board of directors!"

    • **Anita F. Brattina**, President and Owner, Direct Response Marketing, Inc., Pittsburgh, Pennsylvania, and author of the article "The Diary of a Small-Company Owner," appearing in *Inc. Magazine*

"**T**he basic success messages of *Roy's Rules* are so vital to established business owners like me that we would all do well to re-read *Roy's Rules*—year after year.

    • **Stephan W. Ashley**, Owner, The Valley Bookstore, Jackson, Wyoming

Roy's Rules

Guidelines for
Solid Business
Success
and
a Great Life

Roy Jacobson & Herb Henderson

BUSINESS FOCUS PRESS
Dubois, Wyoming

Roy's Rules

Guidelines for Solid Business Success *and* a Great Life

By Roy Jacobson and Herb Henderson

Published by
BUSINESS FOCUS PRESS
P. O. Box 822, Dubois, Wyoming 82513
Phone and FAX (307) 455-2697

This publication is designed to provide accurate and authoritative information in regard to the subject matter covered. It is sold with the understanding that the publisher is not engaged in rendering legal, accounting, or other professional service. If legal advice or other expert assistance is required, the services of a competent professional person should be sought.

ISBN 0-9640244-1-1 (paper)
Library of Congress Catalog Card Number 93-074658

Printed in the United States of America
10 9 8 7 6 5 4 3 2 1

the best to Roger Mayes —

To the hard-working,
results-producing, job-creating
owners of independent businesses,
the heart and soul of
American industry and commerce . . .

May Solid Success Be Yours.

Robert Henderson

Preface

Much of my management consulting career has been devoted to a search for the underlying management principles by which extraordinarily successful businesses operate. I have been particularly intrigued by those elements of management theory and practice that bring success *in the broadest sense* to the owner-operators of independent businesses—producing solid, wealth-producing companies, and the ability of their owners also to enjoy happy, fulfilling and balanced lives. It seemed to me that independent business owners could find solid success through minor adaptations to the professional management theories practiced by major corporations. I was wrong.

Meeting Roy Jacobson was a true revelation to me. As you will read, Roy has been managing his manufacturing company in a way that excites the envy of most entrepreneurs. Not only does Roy's company produce outstanding financial results, but he also finds the time to lead an active, fulfilling life beyond his business activities.

When Roy and I first met in 1989 at his home outside of Phoenix, Arizona, we discussed his business, Southwest Apparel Corporation. Roy is founder and sole owner, and he loves to talk business. He was remarkably open with me, and what he said *lifted me right out of my chair.* He said his primary corporate headquarters was right there in his home. No management team or staff was anywhere to be seen. He told me that he rarely visits his two manufacturing plants in Tennessee. He described the products his company manufactures and sells to major retailing chains—the "cheap shorts" (as they are known in the trade) end of the men's and boys' sportswear business. He told me about being on the road quite often, meeting with customers, suppliers and others who can help his business. His methods of operating seemed a bit bizarre, and I must admit, I had assumed that all products of this type were already being manufactured offshore. I was wrong, again.

Roy then further alarmed me by stating flat-out that he had no interest whatsoever in preparing written business plans, one of my consulting specialties. The idea had crossed my mind that perhaps I could help him develop a winning business plan. So much for that idea! But for someone like me who is steeped in the professional management concepts of business schools and major corporations, the biggest shock was yet to come. I innocently asked Roy, "What are your growth plans for the 1990s?" Seemed like a fair question. Back came a tirade. "Why would I want to grow? To join the ranks of the 'flash-in-the-pan' gang of the 1980s? I'm comfortable where I am. I'm doing fine personally. I have a solid business with no long-term debt—and I'm living a great life. Why would I let growth screw all that up? No way!"

My first thoughts were, "This guy has to be some kind of a kook, or at least a maverick. What about all those icons of my big-corporation past—hands-on management, management-by-walking-around, strategic and operational planning, management and worker team-building, grow or die?"

Several weeks later, Roy had gained enough confidence in me to begin divulging his operating methods and financial status, and how he manages to produce what can only be described as extraordinary results. I learned, for instance, that Roy has been in the garment industry since 1970, founding his manufacturing company, Southwest Apparel, in 1985. Southwest Apparel regularly does about $5 million a year in sales of apparel to major U.S. retailers. *It was profitable its first year in business, and has shown exceptional profits ever since in comparison with the best performing companies in his industry.* Roy has developed sound relations with major retailing organizations, though his company is a very small part of a huge industry. Southwest Apparel produces some of the highest quality products in its industry segment, and it has one of the best balance sheets I have seen in any manufacturing company. Sound asset management, with virtually no debt.

But if these exceptional results weren't enough, what really intrigued me was how Roy lives a much more active and fulfilling life outside of his business than most independent business owners. When something needs to be done, he's right on top of it. Otherwise, he does essentially what he wants to do, when he wants to do it, and has a wonderful time in the process.

The more I got to know Roy, the more I realized that he was accomplishing something pretty darned exceptional, maybe even bordering on the unique. Roy's management principles call for responsibility to family, workers, customers and self, and the solid financial performance of his company that continues, year after year. These are increasingly rare attributes in this hyper era. Some of his principles for success may seem to swim against the tide of conventional wisdom, but there's no doubt that they work extremely well for him. It seemed possible to me that his management principles might work as well for other owners.

Roy and I had extensive and, to me at least, delightful conversations in which we explored in depth the management philosophies that have guided him towards success in business and in life. As a result of these conversations, Roy and I decided to share his business management concepts and methods with other independent business owners, especially owners who have a burning desire to operate financially solid and successful businesses while living balanced and fulfilling lives at the same time.

I assumed responsibility for distilling the essence of Roy's business beliefs into Roy's Rules, twelve powerful guiding principles for independent business owners. Roy's business ideas are so fresh, and his approach to management so unique, that we thought others might enjoy eavesdropping on our question and answer sessions. Thus was born *Roy's Rules*, a lively conversation between a solidly successful, self-taught, robust entrepreneur, and myself, a management consultant with an orientation towards smaller companies who graduated from Harvard Business School and spent much of his business career with major corporations.

Roy's Rules is written primarily for owners and operators of established independent businesses and entrepreneurs aspiring to start new companies. We wouldn't be surprised, however, if corporate executives saw the relevance of Roy's Rules to their own benighted organizations, since many of Roy's ideas are applicable there as well.

The established businesses we had in mind when writing *Roy's Rules* typically employ between ten and 250 people. Their owners are in every conceivable type of business. Collectively, these 900,000 established companies are the very heart and soul of American industry and commerce. These business owners are the guys and gals who are producing the new jobs and expanding the economy, while the big boys keep downsizing and offshoring! Our hope is that by reading *Roy's Rules*, more business owners will be able to say, "I, too, am solidly successful . . . like Roy Jacobson."

Herb Henderson
Dubois, Wyoming

Herb, you're a nice guy, but you talk too much! Come to think of it, that's why we're writing this book together. I needed someone with your background to organize and round out my ideas so that our readers, the owners and future owners of independent businesses, will be suitably impressed and will therefore adapt the success-producing management concepts we describe in *Roy's Rules.* If our readers give them a try, we will have succeeded. If they don't, this is sadly just another "I-did-it-my-way" book.

I've been fortunate during my career to come in contact with many good people along the trail. They helped me, and now it's my turn. American business, particularly its manufacturing base, surely needs all the help it can get!

I began Southwest Apparel with no direct experience or family background in starting, let alone running, a manufacturing business, though I had previously been a successful manufacturers' representative in the apparel field and I felt I knew that industry quite well. I had no fear of starting an apparel company because I could see where major profit opportunities existed for garment manufacturers. I had a good, basic understanding of business management, and I knew I could learn what it takes to make money in manufacturing. That has been my primary focus in running Southwest Apparel—developing a solidly successful company that makes money.

But if that were all there was to it, I think I would have failed. Financial success in business means an awful lot to me, but it sure isn't everything—for me or for anybody. Life is short. Business should be fun. If I can't find a way to live a good life in addition to running my business, I know I'm doing something wrong.

I see so many fine American manufacturing companies and other businesses struggling today to survive in a tough domestic economy, and reeling from the realities imposed by global competition. Opportunities for independently owned companies are out there, especially when you consider the tremendous world and domestic markets that are opening up in front of our eyes. Sure, I made a few good decisions in building my business, but I think many other entrepreneurs could do as well, if not better, if they were to adopt the basic business beliefs that lead to solid success—ideas we present in this book. In my opinion, they spell the difference between average and exceptional results for an independent company, and they make it possible for its owner to lead a great life while running the business. That's the only way to go today! The "flash-in-the-pan," "go-go," "glitzy" companies of the 1980s are mostly history now. Building *solid*, *successful* businesses—that's what business should be all about in the 1990s and beyond.

If readers glean some new thoughts from our book that help them reach their personal objectives, Herb and I will be delighted. Nothing would make us more happy than to add to the ranks of successful, confident and happy business owners. America's owner-operated businesses and their wonderful, hard-working American employees will be a lot better off.

Roy Jacobson
Paradise Valley, Arizona

Contents

1

The Search for Solid Success

If the independent business you own is already as successful as you can imagine it being, and if you are totally at peace with the life you are leading, by all means, don't change a thing. If you feel, on the other hand, that you are not getting all the financial and personal rewards possible from your business, you may want to take a good, hard look at your own ways of doing business, see how they stack up against Roy's Rules, and think about adopting Roy's Rules as your own basic business beliefs.

In the future, independent business owners must learn to react to the realities of the new world economic order, the same realities that are challenging so many of our larger corporate enterprises. Both entrepreneurs and corporate executives must pay attention to the urgent need for global competitiveness, world-class quality and worker productivity, as well as address a whole new demand for responsiveness to customer needs. Independent business owners in particular must find better ways of doing business . . . ways the realities of the global economy dictate business must be conducted today.

As a management consultant, I have the utmost respect for small business owners—the results they produce and the risks they take. I have spent years searching for the guiding management principles that can lead an owner to real success. Not an easy task! The temptation, of course, is to look for clues among the success stories of corporate behemoths. Big mistake! Many of our large industrial corporations continue to downsize in near desperate response to the excruciating realities of global competition and a stagnant economy. Desirable jobs are being lost, and our once secure middle class is hunkering down for what may become an extended battle to regain our competitive edge as a nation and to maintain, let alone expand, the living standards of all our citizens.

The unfortunate fact is that many of our large companies have been doing a lot wrong. Their chief executives operate under a different set of incentives and risks than those of entrepreneurs. They are clearly not providing the right models for independent business owners to follow. I have been forced to come to the sobering realization that large corporations have a tough time helping themselves—let alone providing a blueprint for independent business owners to follow. Their size and complexity, their very mass and inertia, prevent many from doing what they must do to become and remain successful in their own arenas. We need to look elsewhere for exemplars of solid success for business owners.

Small companies—run right—can be big winners

It is now clear to me that the most useful guidelines for small business success must come from within the ranks of small business itself. There are more than 900,000 smaller, independent businesses in the United States, each employing between ten and 250 workers. Together, these companies employ more than 25 million American workers. In many ways, they are the heart and soul of American industry and commerce. Within their ranks are many independent business owners who are exceptional winners—exemplars that others would do well to emulate.

Smaller, simple businesses can have a huge advantage over large, complex corporations when it comes to producing highly successful results. It is equally apparent to me, however, that the most successful independent businesses are being operated according to a set of rules that differ, in many respects, from the latest management theories of the corporate world—the infamous "conventional wisdom." Many learned pronouncements of business "gurus" seem to be better attuned to helping resuscitate moribund corporate bureaucracies than to producing successful results for independent business owners. Highly successful entrepreneurs adopt management methods that are right for their businesses, methods that face the problems and opportunities of the regional, national and world economies realistically. Their methods take full advantage of the many joys of being small and lithe. They demonstrate that *small can be beautiful!*

The sad truth is, however, that too large a number of small businesses have their own crosses to bear. Many come nowhere near to being classified as "world class" when it comes to producing exceptional results for their owners.

Let's face it! How many of today's entrepreneurs are actually realizing the American dream? Most independent business owners are not. They may be eking out a fairly good living, but is that really what they had in mind when they started their enterprises? Are the risks they take justified by the income and wealth they are accumulating? If you, as an independent business owner, are not hitting home runs in your business every week, don't feel bad. Unfortunately, you have lots of company.

In fact, when I take a hard look at our entire population of smaller, entrepreneur-driven businesses, I don't see an entirely pretty picture. What I see today is a wide variety of companies producing widely varying benefits to their owners and to society as a whole. They range from the "Walking Wounded," companies that are on the brink of expiration, to "Ho-Hum" companies that are just getting by, to "Hot-Shot" companies that may be experiencing meteoric growth, but whose very growth may be propelling them right into the dust bin of history.

What are so many business owners doing that is so wrong? What should they be doing to become more successful? Basically, times have changed—dramatically, and many owners haven't changed with the times. No owner can just keep plugging along the old paths, employing the old methods, and hope to have a chance in hell of succeeding. No one! New rules, new ways of doing things apply. That's reality today.

The good news is that a few—a very few—business owners are doing extraordinarily well in today's tough markets. Exemplars for others to follow must exist among their exalted ranks. My goal has been to discover a path to solid, sure success for independent businesses—one that really works. A challenging task!

Owners often hold themselves back

Every entrepreneur is trying to be successful and use that success to lead a satisfying and fulfilling life. Most business owners haven't yet reached that exalted state. Being too focused on the details and missing the big picture is a common problem. Many don't have a clear idea of how or where they should be spending their time, and on what issues. Others aren't tuned in to what their markets are telling them. Some don't know how to react to turbulent trends that are impacting American business enterprise.

These and many other issues are of real concern to most business owners. Because some owners don't have sound conceptual frameworks within which to work out a winning strategy, "Ho-Hum" performance is often the result—in far too many cases. What's missing for many are the basic, proven business beliefs that exemplary business owners use to guide their actions and move their businesses towards real success. Without sound business philosophies that work for smaller companies, floundering is the rule. With them, success—better yet world-class success—can be the reward.

As you probably realize from your own experience, business owners are a persistent, self-confident, driven lot. If they weren't, they wouldn't have chosen the entrepreneurial path in the first place. They have set high goals for themselves, but most keep plugging along without great success, certain that some day soon their ship will come in.

Most owners don't start out with the goal of achieving mediocre results. They would be crazy if they did. The risks are just too high. When fledgling entrepreneurs plunk down all their hard earned savings and go for it, they generally are shooting for the highest achievable level of financial success in their industries. Thank goodness they do, because that's what drives the free enterprise system.

Today, it seems, more and more entrepreneurs are also taking dead aim at a good life—a judicious blend of work, family, fun and outside interests that permits a better, more balanced personal life for business owners. Find an owner who has a stable, profitable business and who uses its financial rewards to underwrite an enviable life-style that provides lots of time for family, friends and fun, and you are staring *solid success* in the face.

Characteristics of a solidly successful company

We all know successful companies. *Solidly* successful companies, however, are a rare breed, and they have certain characteristics that make them stand far above the crowd.

First of all, a solidly successful company is profitable in the extreme and is managed for superior results because its cost structure is among the lowest in its industry. Second, its owner makes highly productive use of his or her time and available assets. Third, the company is *consistently* profitable, making money year after year, in good times and bad. Finally, its cash flow allows its owner to accumulate personal wealth without undermining the financial strength of the business.

These characteristics describe the very type of business I have been searching for. My aim has been to peer inside its owner's brain and uncover the secrets of its success. If I were to discover such an owner, I would have all but solved the mystery of how independent businesses can become *solidly successful*. What an exciting thought!

The solidly successful business owner

Eureka! I've found him! I've found the exemplar that other small business owners may want to emulate on their way to solid success. Let me introduce you to an extraordinarily successful independent manufacturing company, Southwest Apparel Corporation, and its founder and owner, Roy Jacobson. Roy has built a business that is not only competitive, responsive and profitable, but also produces wealth beyond that needed to maintain the financial security of the company itself, even during bad times. Roy fits my description of a solidly successful small business owner to a "t," because he has discovered how to enjoy both solid business success *and* a great life at the same time. And, miracle of all miracles, he is willing to share his management philosophies and methods with the rest of us mortals.

Roy Jacobson—an exemplar of solid success

Roy Jacobson founded Southwest Apparel Corporation in 1985 after spending fifteen years as owner of RMJ Enterprises, a manufacturers' representative firm in the garment industry. Roy's company was profitable its first year, and has shown healthy profits ever since. Southwest Apparel sells approximately $5 million a year of low-priced, men's and boys' sportswear—shorts, tank tops, and sweats—to major U. S. retailing organizations, including Kmart and Sears. The industry refers to these products as "cheap shorts." Southwest Apparel produces some of the highest quality "cheap shorts" in its segment of the sportswear business.

Roy maintains his company headquarters in Paradise Valley, Arizona, a suburb of Phoenix. His two manufacturing plants are located in central Tennessee. His company is a highly profitable player in a huge manufacturing industry, maintaining full, continuous employment and positive cash flow, year after year, even during recessionary times. Just for good measure, Roy's company has an exceptionally solid balance sheet, with virtually no debt.

While building and running his company, Roy has been able to add to his family's estate without diminishing the company's financial strength. He has already firmly established his financial independence through investments made outside the base business.

Most interesting of all, Roy is able to enjoy an active

life beyond his business activities. He makes sure that
time is available for his pursuit of happiness. He flat-out
refuses to let the business run his life or consume all his
time. When something needs to be done, of course, he
is right on top of it. Otherwise, he does essentially what
he wants to do, when he wants to do it. He spends much
more time with his family than the typical business
owner.

Roy makes sure that his company's financial strength
also contributes to the well-being of his employees and
the communities in which they work. Remarkably, he
keeps more than 150 workers gainfully and steadily
employed in Tennessee at better-than-average wages—
in the face of some of the toughest domestic and foreign
competition there is, anywhere.

The personal, family and business goals Roy has set
for himself have supported, even demanded, his
company's solidly successful performance. Roy is a
strong family-man, believing that family and friends come
before all else. His greatest source of business satisfaction
comes from producing "great products," and selling them
to his "great customers." He does not accept being
characterized as "average" or "mediocre" in any aspect of
his life. "Excellence" is the only acceptable outcome. He
feels that his company must perform better than the best,
particularly in the areas of operating costs, profitability,
productivity, cash-generation, stability, and business longevity. Nothing less will do for Roy!

Management principles that challenge the conventional wisdom

I have spent hours, days, yes even weeks with Roy
Jacobson, determined to discover how he achieves such
exceptional results. While doing this, I was struck by the
original twists Roy applies to management principles,

and the extent to which his business philosophies fly in the face of most conventional wisdom. Here is a sampling of Roy's ways of doing things. They may sound foreign to the ears of existing or aspiring business owners, especially if they received basic business training in the hallowed halls of "professionally" managed corporate institutions or graduate business schools:

Concept 1. "Don't hang around the office or plant. Get into the marketplace—out where you need to be."

Concept 2. "Don't spend too much time on your personal computer and spreadsheets. The important numbers must be in your head—all the time."

Concept 3. "Don't even think about growing your business. Think about serving your customers better."

Concept 4. "A written business plan is a useless, even dangerous document. Just say 'no' to formal business plans."

Concept 5. "Business is meant to be fun. Don't let your business run your life."

These seemingly unusual management concepts of Roy's underscore a fundamental point; to become solidly successful, a business owner may need to adopt management philosophies and practices that are shockingly different from those learned in prior years. It may be tough for graduates of large corporations and elite business schools to make the transition from the tenets of "professional" business management to the management concepts of solid success for small business owners. It may be equally difficult for established business owners to adopt new and better ways of doing things. No one said becoming a solidly successful business owner was going to be easy!

The bottom line—exemplary results

I can hear you asking, "How has Roy translated these nice sounding words into solid financial performance—real, money-in-the-bank, exemplary results?" Let me show you the results.

Roy has built his company into a liquid, cash-producing business with financial statements that are considerably more solid than the average garment manufacturer. Just take a look at Southwest Apparel's typical financial performance in comparison with similarly sized companies in the same segment of the U. S. garment industry.

	Industry Average Performance	Typical Southwest Apparel Performance
Operating Expenses		
before Owner Withdrawals	20.0%	5.0%
Current Ratio	1.7:1	2.4:1
Debt/Worth Ratio	1.8:1	0.6:1
Return on Assets Employed	5.7%	9.6%

Now tell me, if these results don't add up to solid success, the solidly successful breed of entrepreneur doesn't exist!

Searching for the path to solid success

The more Roy and I talked, the more it became obvious to both of us that the root cause of his solid success has been his particular set of basic business beliefs, the philosophies and principles he applies when taking management action. They guide his every move and help him make every business decision. They tell him when a proposed policy or operating practice will contribute to the business' success and his own pursuit of happiness, and when it will not. They provide the very foundation upon which his solid success has been built.

After much deliberation, we decided to name Roy's twelve basic business beliefs—"Roy's Rules." Wouldn't you have guessed it?

In the next twelve chapters, Roy and I go one-on-one in intense conversations, trying hard to uncover what Roy's Rules are all about, why they make so much common sense, and how they can help others achieve solid success. You will be able to "listen in" as I badger Roy with some of the questions you might ask him if you had the chance.

I think you will find Roy's frankness both refreshing and challenging. Roy speaks from the heart, and he speaks to business owners from the strength of success and the conviction of proven beliefs. Roy's Rules have helped produce extraordinary results for one independent business owner, Roy Jacobson. They might—they just might—work as well for you.

2

ROY'S RULE NO. 1:

Be in Total Control . . .
at the Helm

PLAYING THE RIGHT ROLES

No one can run your business like you can. You are the entrepreneur who started it. You know where it can and should be going. So take on the important tasks yourself. Don't delegate to others the vital functions that produce solid success. They belong in your personal care—all the time! Don't give up the reins to anybody else. Stay at the helm.

Tell me, Roy, what do you mean by "Being in Total Control . . . at the Helm?"

I mean that the owner of the business must be absolutely, positively in *total control* of the business. He can't let it get away from him for a minute. It's like being the captain of a small ship at sea. The captain obviously has to sleep from time to time. But he sure as hell knows, or ought to know, exactly what is happening with his ship at all times. His mates are primed to give him the latest status report whenever he needs it, or whenever something happens that demands his attention.

When the captain is at the wheel, he is steering the ship and is in total control. There may be times when everyone is down below doing other things. If something happens on deck that needs to be taken care of right away, the captain does it, for heaven's sake. Nothing is beneath him.

Nothing should be beneath a business owner, either. Running a company is just like captaining a ship. You must be in total control all the time, even when you are off having fun. You also need to come to grips with where you are spending your time. You must realize that you can and should be doing many things yourself, more tasks than you previously might have thought proper for a dignified chief executive.

Keep your attention on doing the important things right, yourself. This means being totally obsessed with providing outstanding products and services, being very close to your customers and their needs, and being the lowest-cost producer in your industry. That's how you make money, so that must occupy most of your time and energy. That is where your competitive advantage comes from. All else is secondary. You cannot let others run these crucial aspects of your business. The owner just has to be at the helm—solidly, totally and continuously.

What does an owner do "at the helm?"

To answer that question, consider why entrepreneurs start businesses in the first place. They have a burning desire to create something, to venture out on their own, for whatever reason. Entrepreneurs have a natural tendency to see opportunities in whatever they are doing. So they create something that is likely to satisfy a real need, they get some money together, and they do it.

Think about that. Isn't that what you did? *You* did it!
You saw the possibilities and the opportunities, and *you*
did it. It just wouldn't have worked unless you were
completely in charge—completely at the helm. You had
a clear picture of what you were trying to do—a vision of
what your company could become in the future. Now, of
course, adjustments are usually made along the way so a
company can hit its targets. But no one should be at the
helm except the owner, because you are the only one
who has the complete picture of where the company can
and should be going.

It may sound over-simplified, but the basic job of the
owner, first and foremost, is really just to make money by
doing things right. To make this happen, owners should
put themselves in charge of the management tasks that
are the most important—the ones that *must* be done right.
Those tasks are what I call the "externals," the management activities that deal with the things that impact the
business from the outside. They include discovering and
taking advantage of customer needs and other profit
opportunities, positioning the company for market advantage, getting products to market, knowing what is
going on in the outside world—particularly industry
trends, and being in close touch with suppliers and
external financing sources. Owners need to spend a lot
of time in the field doing these things. No one else can put
the right spin on them.

The owner at the helm also better have grease under
his fingernails. That's what "hands-on" management
really means. Take on the most important tasks yourself—you can do them better than anyone else. But be
willing to do just about anything that will improve your
company's fortunes. Don't fall into the trap of thinking
that for every new task that needs doing, you have to add
a new body to the staff. You can save a tremendous
amount of unnecessary management and staff salaries by
assigning new tasks to your existing staff—*including to*

yourself.

Personally, I have no time for owners who spend all their time massaging their PC spreadsheets and turning out plan after business plan. It may be fun, but it's an exercise in futility, and it doesn't make money for you. Those spreadsheet numbers that look so right can easily be dead wrong if you're not completely focused on the real results your company is generating. It's much better for the owner of a smaller business to be out in the field on top of customers and profit opportunities, determining where the company is going. By communicating these findings frequently with the management team to get their valued input and to keep everybody working together, the owner, the management team, and the company itself become its own business plan. The "plan" must be in the owner's head, where it can be worked and reworked every day with help from the management team.

Owners make money one order at a time, one week at a time, one opportunity at a time. Owners of independent businesses must focus on making money *now*. Tomorrow won't do. It's gotta be *now*. You may get someone, or a group of people, to assist you in any of these areas, but you must never delegate total responsibility for doing the crucial job of making money to anyone. It's the owner's job. It's your job. It's gotta be *you!*

Don't delegate?
That's contrary to everything
I ever learned about management, Roy.

Look, there's a difference between being at the helm, and getting help or assistance in running your business. *Just don't delegate the responsibility for making money.* Don't allow anyone else to make the vital decisions. You, the owner, are the best one to do it, and you shouldn't need a lot of help. If you can't or won't do it yourself, then you shouldn't be the owner of your company. You'd better get out, fast!

Of course, if you grow your company to the point where you are running multiple operations as top dog, you'll be dealing with broader management issues, like developing people, and all that other BS that will eventually top you out. But for owners who want to run successful smaller companies and put aside a little money for their families, a wonderful life awaits them if they run their companies right. And by "right," I mean not being afraid to do all the vital, the truly important, things yourself.

If you're doing so many of the important things yourself, what kind of a management team do you need?

Most smaller businesses just don't need very many managers. You really ought to be your own Chief Sales Officer, Chief Marketing Officer, Chief Financial Officer, Chief Product Development Officer, and even your own Controller. I am. When you take on the most important management functions yourself, you don't need many other managers hanging around, sopping up overhead dollars. By assuming these vital functions, more rewards can be distributed to you and to your small management team.

Frankly, in a small or medium-sized business, the owner can pretty much run the whole show with little help.   Work on keeping your management team small, tightly knit and close to you. You don't need to see them every day, but you sure ought to talk to each one every day. That keeps the need for meetings down. Staff meetings are a total waste of time. I have no use for them.

My company, Southwest Apparel, which has about 150 employees, has only two top managers, including myself, plus an administrator and eight line supervisors. That's it. That's all we have and all we need. We are one small, single-minded, highly-focused management team. There's no need for teams within the management team, let alone organization charts or job descriptions. My management team has broad responsibilities to get the company's work done right. They know their jobs. They know what the company is trying to accomplish overall. Anything more sophisticated or complicated is overkill— and overkill takes money out of my pockets.

Since owners should be working their rear ends off on the "externals," they'd better be on the road a good bit of the time. That means a trusty lieutenant is required to mind the store and work the "internals" in your absence. I prefer having an operations manager—a very good one. Once my operations manager proved to me that he could get the "internals" job done right, I was able to spend most of my time in the field making big opportunities happen. If your operations manager is not so great, you've got a problem because you'll have to watch over operations really carefully. That takes away from your basic job— making money for your company.

Which reminds me. I have a theory that says business owners usually spend their time doing what they think they do best. For example, if you came up the manufac- turing route before forming your own company, you'll probably spend most of your time looking over manufac- turing. You'll probably be a great production manager, but a lousy owner. And the business may suffer because of it.

If you own the business, you have no choice. You've got to look outward, sensing where the opportunities are, and making them happen. You can find others to get the internal jobs done.

If you take on the vital jobs yourself, you should have

little need for outside advisors. Of course, you probably need to have an outside accounting firm, though that even goes against my constitution. But look out for financial advisors who want to take you public or some other foolish idea. They want to make money for themselves, not for you.

As for management consultants, God forbid! Running a solidly successful business isn't all that tough. If you started it, and you are running it hands-on, you can make a big success of it. You know so much more about your business than consultants do, just tell them to take a hike when they come around. Spend that money on your next road trip, really listening to customers, digging up some great opportunities, and making money.

Why would an entrepreneur ever be tempted to give up being in total control?

That always amazes me! When an owner's business grows to a certain point, the owner suddenly feels an uncontrollable urge to get advice from someone else. Maybe that's happened to you. You read about something you think you ought to be doing, and you conclude that maybe it's wise to relinquish some of your duties and create a staff to help you do these wonderful things. You suddenly feel you can't run the company without all this outside wisdom that wasn't there when you started the business.

This never made any sense to me. The best person to be at the helm, I feel, is the entrepreneur who started the whole thing. Owners really need to drown out the chorus of advisors telling them that somehow, when their companies reach seven figures, they are no longer able to be at the helm without three or four assistants to tell them which way to go. The position achieved from those monumental efforts expended by the entrepreneur during start-up, the first two to five years of hard work and dedication, should not be relinquished or compromised. You have to stay there, in the saddle. Stay at the helm, and don't be tempted to turn over the real running of the business to anyone. You know what is best for your company. You are the one person who is going to make it successful. No one else can do that for you.

What risks do owners run if they are not at the helm all the time?

Trying to use managers or staff members to really run your business, make key decisions, manage your cash flows, take over your product development, or do other essential duties can be disastrous. You have to stay really close to your products, your cash positions, your banking relationships, and your customer relationships—nothing is more important.

If you let anyone else actually run your business, you run the risk of losing your company rapidly in today's economy. Some say it's hard to kill a company. Not true! It happens all the time, especially when the owner thinks it is finally safe, and he or she no longer has to be at the helm. In the 1990s, the margins are smaller and the competition is greater, so room for error just doesn't exist. If you try delegating this vital stuff, you might turn around and all of a sudden, it's gone! All that effort you put in starting your business isn't recoverable. Sorry!

I've seen it happen, time after time. A company has a few good years and right away the owner hires a sales manager, delegates most of the customer-interface stuff, and stops visiting customers regularly. The owner reads reports of what customers are buying. All these reports look great. Two or three quarters go by before the owner knows there's a problem. Then, all of a sudden, there's a cash crunch. The company is in the tubes, and the owner doesn't know it.   The owner asks the controller, "How come?" "But! But!" the controller responds.   Well, those "buts" happen because *the owner was not at the helm!* That company is history!

Roy, give me an illustration. Maybe that will help nail down your point.

Several years ago, before I founded Southwest Apparel, I was invited to attend a meeting at the offices of a "Big 8" accounting firm in New York City by a company for which I was a manufacturers' representative at the time. We were visiting what they called their "Emerging Business" division, which specialized in helping young businesses grow.   I was a little intimidated by the long elevator ride up to the forty-eighth floor and all the fancy, dark woodwork in their offices.

I recall going into their big board room to join all these financial guys.   The company's business had recently grown from $5 to $11 million in annual sales.   I wasn't sure why I was there.   The manufacturing company's financial department and controller were there, as well as the owner and his management staff.   They had brought enormous amounts of paperwork, charts, graphs and pro forma projections. The business had been very profitable at $5 million.   Now, they were losing money at $11 million.   At the time, I was selling $8 million of product at a 5% commission.   That's $400,000 a year for me.   Not a bad deal!

The company had projections that indicated they would make money the next year if they could reach $12 million in sales.   I think they kind of fabricated all those numbers, because they never made any sense to me.   It looked like the company president had gotten himself hooked on doing spreadsheets and never left his office. The problem was the spreadsheets. They were totally out of touch with reality; with what was going on in the marketplace. A ridiculous exercise.

All the guys present acted as if they knew just about everything, but it turned out they had not written the Bible. Both the company financial guys and the "Big 8" guys were telling the president about all the good things that were going to happen. Of course, the company was paying a couple hundred grand per year for their financial department, and the outside accountant fees were maybe $65,000 per year for their review. Remember, this was the "Emerging Business" division of the "Big 8" accounting firm—providing expensive services so companies could emerge!

All these high paid people were sitting in the board room talking about the projections, and I was thinking to myself that this is a lot of crap. The owner was there, surrounded by all his advisors, and there I was, the guy who sells most of the company's products, who goes to the factory once a month, and who makes most of the money. I was looking at stacks of papers, graphs and all these meaningless, make-work reports. I looked at the owner, and I could tell that he wasn't all that sure about such positive projections, either.

It occurred to me, if the company wasn't making any money at $11 million in sales, why didn't it drop back to $5 million and start over? I was willing to give up some of my commission on the higher sales—give up a couple hundred grand to make this company profitable again. But scaling down would not support a big financial staff, nor would it support the "Big 8" consultants who worked in the "Emerging Business" division.

Here was an $11 million company, losing money, and the owner had worry written all over his face. When I started selling for them, the owners were making a nice living, as was I. Now the company was in trouble and both of these groups of financial types—*advisors*—were going to come up with a solution. They were going to grow the company out of its profit problems.

This owner had gone the way of many owners who finally make it. He had been enjoying big success after many years of struggle. He had built a solid company. The company had no debt. It did a few million bucks in sales each year. The owner made a nice living. The company kept growing because it did a nice job for its customers.

Then, all of a sudden, the company went from $5 to $11 million. That involved bringing on board a lot of management people. Bigger staffs. More advisors. More overhead. The owner paid $900,000 for New Jersey offices that never transmitted anything to the bottom line. All cost. No profit. The owner had lost control. He had lost it!

The company died, of course, in Chapter 11.

The significance of your story, Roy?

I'm sure there are a lot of companies that have "emerged" from the "Emerging Business" division, but the company I worked with sure as hell was not one of them!

My point is that *the owner should have stayed at the helm.* When his first "assistant" came on board and gave him a set of recommendations in a report, he should have said, "This doesn't make any sense to me. Why should we be doing this? Why should I start up a new plant? Why should I buy an office building? Why should I buy another company? Why? Why? Why?"

The significance of the story? I've seen too many disasters like the one I've described, disasters that happened because the owner stopped being at the helm in total control. If you have a good thing going, and your company is profitable, damn it, hold on to control and be skeptical of all advisors. If you, the owner, don't understand something your advisors are telling you, think twice—think thrice. It just might not make any sense! Think it through yourself. Make your own decisions. Trust the same instincts that got you to your current position in the first place. Don't let people come in and take over your business. Don't give up the reins. *Stay at the helm!*

The Quick-Study Guide for Independent Business Owners

BE IN TOTAL CONTROL . . . AT THE HELM

• Be in total control of the business . . . absolutely and positively, all the time. Operate the business yourself—hands on.

• Focus *all* of your energy on making money . . . providing outstanding products, being close to your customers, and being the low-cost producer. You cannot delegate these fundamental responsibilities to anyone.

• Take charge of the "externals" yourself; markets, customers, financing, suppliers and especially big new opportunities. They spell the difference between average and exceptional performance.

• Keep your management team very small, very good, very motivated, and very well integrated with your vision for the company.

• Hire an outstanding operations manager to run the "internals," allowing you time to concentrate your efforts on the "externals."

• Don't spend too much time on formal business planning. Operate so that your vision, your management team, and the company *are* the plan.

• Be wary of advisors. You can figure it out for yourself! Get people to help you if you must, but don't let others come in and run your business. *Don't give up the reins! Stay at the helm!*

3

ROY'S RULE NO. 2:

Get Into the Market

CREATING PROFIT OFPORTUNITIES

Get out of your office! Get into the field! That's where you belong much of the time. It's in the vital "externals" of the business—markets, customers, business opportunities, market and product positioning, suppliers and financing sources—where you, and only you, can really find out how to serve your customers best, seize profit opportunities, and make money.

Roy, what's "getting into the market" all about?

Owners who are really "at the helm" spend most of their time absorbed with whatever is truly essential to making money. That means you are bearing down, all the time, on providing outstanding products and services, being close to your customers, and doing whatever it takes to be the lowest-cost producer in your industry. Now, being the lowest-cost producer certainly involves how a business is organized and structured and how it handles its various cost elements. This part of managing is mainly "internal" work. The other two important

factors, however, having great products and being close
to your customers, obviously require a lot of effort on
your part that is outside the walls of the office or shop, no
matter what the industry.

Owners needs to "get into the market" personally in
order to deal with all the "external" influences that
strongly affect the success of any company. When
owners are out in the market, taking on all those gorillas,
they are doing much more than personally selling their
products or services. They are also discovering product
needs and other profit opportunities, positioning the
company for maximum advantage in the marketplace,
getting products to market the best way possible, staying
in tune with market trends, and maintaining solid relations with suppliers and financing sources.

How well you and your company deal with that
"external" world will make or break your business. To do
that, you need to be out in the field a large part of your
time. If you aren't, I doubt you'll ever be solidly successful.

Why is it so important that the owner actually be in the marketplace?

It just makes sense. Owners who are very close to the
market can do a better job of making money than those
who spend all their time in a laboratory designing the
latest-and-greatest new product, or in the factory turning
out lots of widgets. Owners who can read their customers' needs, and understand what they really want, are
better able to push their products and resources in
directions that will give them a big advantage competitively.

That doesn't mean that an owner, for example, whose
whole background has been in accounting can't do the
job. There are many examples of former accountants

who did a complete flip and actually turned out to be great entrepreneurs.

Whatever your background, training and business experience have been, your know-how will be useful to you in running a successful company. But your involvement in the key elements of running a *highly successful* business absolutely can't stop there. You cannot concentrate only on those things with which you are familiar and which you do best. No matter how difficult it may be for you to change your habits, you must get out into the marketplace and start listening. If you listen well, the market will tell you exactly what you ought to be doing to satisfy customer needs and to design and produce the right products. Then, if you can organize and direct your company to turn those wonderful hints into reality, you're on the right track.

Everything is changing so very fast in today's markets. Industries are in varying degrees of turmoil, and the needs of customers are shifting quickly. Miss a few of these turns in the road, and your company's history. It's just not good enough to rely entirely on your marketing and sales organization to provide you with the kind of market intelligence necessary to survive and prosper.

An owner, also, can't get away with just making an occasional sales call with a salesman. If you are out there in the marketplace enough of the time, the marketplace will tell you where it wants to be going. It's not a big deal to pull this information out of the market. Seek and search. Just be there, and listen! It's no big deal. You don't have to be clever to get this feedback. Just be out there, be receptive, and let the market direct you.

Many owners I know have a certain awe of markets. Markets can be a real mystery to them, frankly because they are not that close to where their products are being used. They prefer to let their marketing and sales organizations do most of that work. Bad idea!

Owners have to blast through the "mystery" thing, and

get into the action themselves. Their fear of markets reminds me of the Wizard of Oz—the scene where Dorothy and the gang are ushered in to see the Wizard. They see an awesome display of props and lights, smoke and mirrors designed to impress and intimidate anyone who dares enter. They are all scared, until they peek behind the screen, and what do they find? There's the Wizard, fumbling around doing the best he can. He's an ordinary guy, just trying to do his job, and probably damned interested in getting help from anyone he can.

Markets are a lot like that. Look behind the screen, and you see ordinary people who need all the help they can get to do their jobs better. Just rub shoulders with your customers, and their customers—the end users. They will be impressed to meet the owner, and you will learn so much by actually being there, taking in everything, including orders.

How important is it to be out there personally—in the marketplace? Let me be blunt. If you spent all of your time last week, Monday through Friday—8 to 12 hours a day, in your office, *don't ever, ever, ever do that again!* Get the hell out of your office. I don't care if you go for a walk in the park. Hopefully, you will go visit a customer. Or you will go see where your product is being used, or you will go talk to the people that you hope will use your product. But get the hell out of the office! Get it?

OK, I've got it. So I'm out there in the market. What do I do now, Roy?

Of course, a basic reason for owners to be out in the market is the constant search for new sales opportunities—ways to make a buck. A sales force or manufacturers' reps can move a lot of iron, or course, but an owner must be out there with them.

Regardless of background or interests, the owner must be the chief marketeer and salesman of the company—there's no other way. You may have a marketing manager or a sales manager, but you have the fundamental marketing and sales responsibilities for your company. If you own the business, you just can't shake those responsibilities.

Also, you ought to work some of your customers alone, at all levels—probing, questioning, getting to know their feelings about your company, and understanding where their needs are going before they even realize it. Is this difficult? No, not really. It's amazing what owners can accomplish when they get out of the office and into the marketplace.

For example, I have been successful at going back to customers to make favorable price adjustments or quantity and delivery adjustments. Nothing is cast in concrete! Even purchase orders. I was always told that customers never changed their procedures. Not true. If you keep good working relationships with your customers, you can work things out. You, the owner, just have to get out there and keep trying. It's easier and more productive for the owner to do it than anyone else.

Roy, how crucial is it to have a strong market position?

I've always felt that market position is really about how your customers look at you—how much they respect you and your products. I think most business owners have a pretty good gut feeling that tells them if they have a strong market position—or if they don't. If a company doesn't have a solid market position, it has a hell of a time getting the attention of its potential customers. They couldn't care less whether you existed or not. When you enjoy a good position, your customers really do care about you, because you are doing something for them that makes their lives a whole lot better. Like providing quality products that sell easily, and good, responsive customer service.

One thing I know for sure. Your company will never be a solid success until it has earned a solid position in the eyes of its customers. When your company has it, it no longer has to fight it out every inch of the way on price or some other going-nowhere factor. And, having a strong market position has nothing to do with the size of a company, or its share of the market. *Smaller, independent businesses can attain strong market positions.* Southwest Apparel has, because my customers like the way I do business.

Owners must take the lead in building a strong market position. They can't delegate this task very well, because it has to do with deciding on the markets their companies should be targeting, and the products or services that are right to serve those customers. It also has to do with producing positive cash flow for their companies. Those decisions are far too important and interrelated to be left to a damn committee, no matter how skilled and experienced its members may be. The owner has to be in the middle of this all the time.

Owners, of course, can't make these positioning decisions in a vacuum. The whole world is changing. Suppliers are changing their materials or their pricing or their availability. Customers are moving on to new products and newer versions of the same basic products, like the fashion changes in my markets.

Basically, you need to provide what your markets are looking for at price levels that mean good profits for your company, but that make it difficult for competitors to match you comfortably. Two factors really count. First, provide what they want. You can do this only if you are personally very close to your customers. Second, make sure that your company is able to produce the product or service at an attractive price to the customer, but also one that makes money for the company. Making good money happens when your company's direct and overhead costs are the lowest in its field. If you can turn out products that customers really want at prices they are willing to pay and make good money at the same time, you're on your way to a strong market position.

Consistent quality is also a big factor. Today everyone expects high quality from all products and services. If you don't measure up, you're history. Here's what buyers are saying to you; "Can you *consistently* produce products or services of the highest quality? And, by the way, I'm not going to spend an extra dime for consistently high quality, because it just has to be there. Period."

To develop a strong market position, the job of the owner boils down to this. You must make product, market, service and capability decisions that result, in the final analysis, in earning an identity in the eyes of your customers that makes them want to do business with you—now, next year, and beyond. If you can do that and also be highly profitable, *that's* what I call having a strong market position!

Roy, how do your competitors figure in all of this?

Frankly, I never give competitors a second thought. I'm just not interested! This may shock you, but face it! Why should I? I'm doing good business with great customers, and making all the money I need. In a real sense, I *am* the competition. And that's the way I want to keep it. If I lay awake at night, it's only to think through how I can better serve my customers, and not because I'm worried about what my competitors are doing or not doing. I keep up on what is going on in my industry, so I won't get caught by surprise competitive moves. But that's it.

I'm convinced that many owners spend far too much time thinking and worrying about the competition. If you must be worrying about something, worry about how to be the best and lowest cost supplier in your industry. That will take care of the competition. You'll be the leader that the others are trying to catch. You'll *be* the competition!

What types of products and markets should an independent company go after?

I believe a small, independent company can develop a strong market position in just about any industry, as long as its products aren't too complex. Look at my company, Southwest Apparel. My industry is loaded with much larger suppliers and many small manufacturers. But I'm doing just fine.

Now, I wouldn't recommend starting a company to produce jumbo jets, especially if you want to be in control of your company and your life. Some markets are obviously a lot more desirable than others. Selecting the best one depends on your interests, your competence, your experience, and even what you like to do. In my case, I knew the garment business inside and out from my years as a manufacturers' rep. I could see profit opportunities in garment manufacturing, and I really loved the business. That's why I started Southwest Apparel.

My feeling is that independent business owners are a hell of a lot better off producing and selling products that are what I call "pull" products. Those are products the need for which is well known and well established—like the "cheap shorts" I produce. If owners can improve upon the norm of their industries, enhancing their products or the services provided, they can move into a solid market position without a lot of grief. If, on the other hand, they go after "push" products—products that require a big market development effort from scratch, owners are bound to have a really tough time convincing customers they need what they are trying to sell. They will also find it more difficult to establish solid relations with their customers.

Of course, no matter what you are selling, if you have a passion for your products and the markets you are serving, you have a much better shot at market strength than the owner who is in it just for the money. The chances of the latter making it are between nil and none.

So there you are, out in the market trying to sell your famous widgets to the heflump industry. The question comes up, "Should I concentrate my guns on a small part of that total market—the famous 'specialty products for a niche market'—or should I go for basic products that serve a broad need?" I'm convinced that niche markets often *seem* to be a good way to get started. But, let's be realistic. If the niche market selected is any good for making money, you can bet your bottom dollar there will be plenty of contentious competitors in that market with you in no time at all. Look at what happened to neighborhood video stores, for example. That particular "niche" lasted maybe one or two years, then everybody was in it. So why not just pay a lot of attention to supplying a great, basic product to a few customers that really like your style? That approach can work just as well, and often it's a lot better for many independent businesses than niche marketing.

I should warn you, though, about "fickle" markets. These are the markets that just don't seem to be able to make up their minds about what products they want from year to year, or even month to month. A good example of a "fickle" market is one that consumes high technology products. The rate of technology change is so fast that the typical life cycle for many high tech products is less than two years. You heard me right—less than two years!

How can anybody make any money in that type of business? The answer is simple. Few do. I certainly wouldn't want to bet my money on that questionable a venture. I'm interested in making money for myself, not feeding the money merchants!

You may ask, though, "Isn't the fashion business the most fickle of all markets?" You've got me there. It is. But, if you concentrate on the basic products that are bought by the masses year after year, and stay very close to the latest fashion trends, you can make it work. Every once in a while, I do indulge myself and agree to make a garment that one might call "high fashion." The risks are high, but—hallelujah!—the gross margins are better. As long as I keep that high-risk stuff under twenty percent of my total production, I'm willing to take the gamble from time to time.

I've always felt that most companies should fight to gain market-share dominance. Roy, what are your thoughts on that?

The question always comes up, "What about pushing for market share, or broadening the market base?" These are really the same thing. The question should be, "How many customers should my company have?" I'll admit to being a contrarian on this subject. To me, the more customers you have, the more potential headaches you have to endure. Headaches, and problems, and risks. When you are pushing for a large market share, you are obviously going to have to take on every possible customer. A few will turn out to be great customers, but more of them will turn out to be sources of lots and lots of headaches. Credit risks—that sort of thing.

I believe that having a highly diversified customer base can be injurious to a company's health, especially if its owner wants it to be a solidly successful independent business. Even though I have about a hundred customers now, I'd just as soon see that number *fall*. I would prefer to sell more products to other departments of my existing great customers' organizations. I know these customers very well. They like doing business with me. They pay their bills on time. I would probably be a lot better off by being more selective and reducing my customer base, while increasing the number of individual buyers and departments that I do business with at each customer. It's a strategy worth considering. I'll have to try it!

At one point I got lots of free advice from bankers and consultant friends who told me that too large a percentage of my business was coming from too few customers. So what did I do? I added some new customers. What a mistake! They didn't help my bottom line because of all the extra headaches and cost to service. I realize now that I should have refocused my efforts on fewer, rather than on more accounts, and told all those experts who were so free with their advice to shove it!

Roy, how about moving into new markets?

Dangerous. Very dangerous. I have no problem coming up with new products that I can sell to my existing customers. Say, ladies' shorts, in my case. As long as the new product isn't too different from my present products, and it can be sold to the same customers, why not? If the new product fits the identify I have built so carefully for my company, it might make a lot of sense.

But if the idea is to start selling my products to a whole new market where I don't know the customers, and they don't know me, that's a different story. That could create a whole new set of problems that could really hurt. My point is, once a business has established a strong market position within an established market, stick to it! As they say, stick to your knitting. Resist the temptation to move into uncharted waters. If you have a solid source of cash flow, protect it, and build on it.

I have an unbreakable law on this subject. *Don't mess with the money source.* I'll never ignore my base business and get into something I'm not really good at.

If, as an owner, you have the time, money and inclination to start a whole new venture to take advantage of an unbelievable opportunity, fine. Set a pile of bucks aside, and have at it. But be prepared to lose it all, because you probably will.

Whatever you do, don't, please don't, mess with your main source of income. Messing with your money source is a fool's way to mess up a wonderful market position and a thriving business.

What about coming up with new product designs?

I believe that when you, the owner, are out in the field, you *are* the company's research and development department. Or, at the very least, you are the company's "new product definition" department. You can find out about consumer needs that could be satisfied with new products. Or you might find out about feasible refinements to existing products that could increase sales. By listening to customers, owners can do a better job of product definition than anyone else.

Particularly with smaller businesses, the only way to find out about a product, how people look at it and what it should be, is by the owner being out in the marketplace. In many companies, engineers design the products. These companies just don't get good information on what customers really want. Owners are the best ones to define products, but only when they are very close to their customers. Picking the right products and services to sell to customers is a key part of market positioning. Your company may already have access to certain technologies that give it something different to offer to your customers. You have to stay on top of what is happening with technology in your industry in order to keep from being blind-sided by a dramatic new development. But dramatic shifts in basic technologies are pretty darn rare. It's hard to kill an established technology. People are probably still buying old-style germanium semiconductors, for all I know. Let the huge companies struggle with bringing out the latest technologies. Most business owners will learn about it in plenty of time to make the shift, if they ever need to. It's much better to concentrate on understanding the customers' needs and wants that can be satisfied with today's technologies, and then find out how to make it with the lowest possible direct and overhead costs. Do that, and you win!

Another thing owners can do in the field is to get direct feedback on how well their present products are performing, especially if customers are having problems with their products. Owners never want to lose customers. That's a cardinal sin, no matter what you make. Whether a company makes toilet plungers or provides a cleaning service, losing customers is tough, because they're too hard to come by.

The real test of how effective you are in the market is how you deal with a customer crisis that involves one of your products. The best way to deal with that situation, in my opinion, is to get on an airplane and go visit the customer, even if it means making an unscheduled trip. Then do whatever it takes to resolve the problem. When an owner gets on a horse and fixes the problem fast, that customer will surely remember such an extraordinary company and its owner.

Close customer contact also puts an owner in a strong

position to determine the right pricing levels for new products—levels that maximize volume and gross profits. I'm always amazed how often customers will tell me what the right price levels must be in order to be competitive. They would probably never tell a salesman this information, but they seem only too willing to talk "business" with an owner who has developed a strong relationship. Owners can feel comfortable asking, "What's it going to take to get your business?" And they'll probably get good answers.

What are your thoughts, Roy, on moving products to market?

When owners develop an idea for a business, they end up with a product or service that must be channeled, eventually, to an end consumer. Some owners may find it best to sell their products or services direct to end consumers through retail stores or mail order. Others channel products through as many as three steps of distribution before their goods get into the hands of end users. Whatever your particular situation, you need to keep checking with direct and indirect customers at all levels to see if there aren't better ways of reaching your ultimate customer, the end consumer.

Some companies have their own direct sales forces, but most sell through distributors, or they sign up manufacturers' representatives—a commission-only sales force. I was a manufacturers' representative before I started Southwest Apparel, so I'll never knock reps. They are among the most important people in my world. Typically, however, owners and sales managers have to work with them continuously. They consume a lot of your time. A word of caution. Owners can spend a lot of time giving classes on their products to reps and trying to work out effective marketing programs, just to broaden the base of customers—which may or may not be the wise thing to do. In many cases it is easier, and a heck of a lot more productive and efficient, for the owner to go out and book business, especially when large, important accounts are involved. Then the direct sales force or your manufacturers' representatives can be used to augment your own direct sales efforts. This approach saves money and keeps you in the marketplace—where you belong.

Roy, how do you keep on top of industry trends?

I always make a point to talk business, especially about what's going on in my industry, with everyone I run into while I'm in the market making sales calls or dealing with suppliers. I talk to customers, prospects, vendors, bankers—even hotel clerks and cabbies. By listening to everyone I see while in the field, I pick up on trends in my industry that could either help me in the future, or end up biting me in the tail. Try doing the same on your next field trip.

Reading trade magazines helps, but there's no substitute for person-to-person exchanges out in the real world. If you're really in the market, listening, your company may not need to attend industry conventions or commission expensive studies, just to pick up industry intelligence. You will already know, from first hand exposure, what's going on in your field.

Why should owners want to stay in close touch with their support organizations?

Owners also should visit their more important vendors while in the field. They are a terrific source of market intelligence. Try having a vendor travel with you and make sales calls on customers. They can get behind your sales programs in many ways, including selling their product to you at a price that will allow both of you to get the business. The ideal would be to create a partnership among the customer, your company and your vendors. Vendors can even help close the business by providing special arrangements that make the contract exclusive to you.

Vendors are meant to call on *their* customers. Reverse that tradition, and you'll be surprised how much help they can be in opening up new profit opportunities with *your* customers.

One of my good fortunes in life has been never getting along too well with bankers. But I never let that get in the way of building solid relationships with my money sources. They say, never surprise your banker, and I certainly subscribe to that advice. I like to hand-deliver my latest quarterly financial statements, so I can explain the numbers to them, and let them know how they can help me in the future. They really appreciate the attention. Few owners bother. That's a big mistake. A banker can be a business owner's best friend and supporter, but only if you "water his garden." So, while you're out in the marketplace, stop in and see "Lonesome George," your loan officer. You, too, can learn to love a banker!

Frankly, Roy, how well has Southwest Apparel been doing in its markets?

Of course, there are hundreds of apparel manufacturers in the United States, and who knows how many offshore garment manufacturers. I specialize, as you know, in men's and boys' sportswear. I'm a tiny player, though I'm selling my products to the big folks—the major mass retailers, like Kmart and Sears. Southwest Apparel sells to about a hundred accounts, with the majority of my products going to a few big ones. I spend most of my time in the field with the big accounts, and that seems to help. I listen to their buyers, and I pay a lot of attention to what they want produced. We're able to provide a quality product at a low price—because of our low cost structure. That gets the job done for us.

Our customers really do seem to prefer to do business with Southwest Apparel. That doesn't mean they just throw business our way. We still have to earn every dime we get, and work hard to keep their business. But the mutually-supportive relationships we've developed with our major accounts have given us a really strong market position.

We have also developed a strong identity in the eyes of our customers, and that has really strengthened our market position. They think of Southwest Apparel as a reliable and low-cost manufacturer of basic fashions for men and boys. That's my product and market positioning, and it's worth a lot to me. I never want to do anything that will compromise or jeopardize that identity.

That's Southwest Apparel—a maker of good, cheap shorts sold to mass markets through mass retailers. That consistent identity has played a major role in making my company solidly successful.

It all boils down to listening to the marketplace on its turf, doesn't it, Roy?

Yes. By doing that, owners will not only find new sales opportunities, but they can define product refinements that have real market appeal, or even see the need to create new products. I recall once visiting a major account and walking down the hallway, saying "hi" to everyone, as I always do. I happened to walk into the office of a man I was not even doing business with, and he was busy working on a new product. I asked what it was. He said it was the latest version of a similar children's playwear product they were already selling. I said, "Hey, that's great. I wish you a lot of success."

I proceeded down the hall, took a right turn and went into my scheduled meeting with the company's purchasing department, ready to close a deal on our regular business. As the meeting was concluding, I said, "By the way, I understand you have been doing some work on a new children's playwear item." They were impressed with my new knowledge. I said, "We would like to submit some samples, and see if we could get an order." Before I left town three days later, we had received an order for the new line worth several hundred thousand dollars.

When I walked in the building, I was totally unaware of my customer's interest in that new product. I was definitely not aware of the position it was suddenly taking in the marketplace. I made this discovery from someone I just knew casually. He was really not a buyer of my products—not one with whom I usually dealt. I had just dropped in to do a little "catharsing," because I believe that everyone is a potential customer and opportunities can be found anywhere.

The final result was that I was able to turn a new, undeveloped situation into an order for a whole new product we had never made before. That's what "getting into the market" can do for you. It *creates opportunities.*

The point is—the business opportunities are out there, in the market. Right?

This story illustrates my belief that owners must get out into the market, always stirring up new opportunities, and getting feedback. The point is, one never knows where the opportunities are. Some are happening right now.

If you want to create opportunities, you sure as hell are not going to find them sitting in your office. I know where they *aren't*—they're not there in your office. *The only place they are is in the market!* We still make the new children's playwear item today. Southwest Apparel has shipped a couple million bucks worth to date. One of my suppliers was with me at the time. She still chuckles about it, saying, "Roy went in Door A a 'dummy,' and came out Door C an 'expert.' And he never left the building." That's an opportunity seized. What should an owner be doing out there in the marketplace? *Seizing profit opportunities!*

The Quick-Study Guide
for Independent Business Owners

GET INTO THE MARKET

- One of a business owner's main jobs is to be out in the market, seizing profit opportunities, building a market position, and creating a strong identity with customers.
- While there, work on the "externals"—marketing, sales, product definition, industry and market trends, distribution channels, vendors, and financing sources.
- Having a strong market position does not depend on a company's size, number of customers, or market share.
- For less risk, position your company to produce a relatively known product that has an established need. Be better at producing and selling that product than anyone else. Save the pioneering for others.
- Having a broad customer base does not necessarily minimize risk or build market position. You can limit yourself to a few exceptional customers and still be strongly positioned in your markets.
- Do more questioning and listening than selling and telling.
- Don't worry too much about competitors. Focus on serving your customers better. *Be* the competition.
- Smaller companies can develop strong positions in broad markets for basic products. You don't have to limit yourself to niche products or niche markets.
- Once you have established a strong market position in your present markets, resist the temptation to move into entirely new markets.
- Basic Rule: Don't mess with the money source. Stick to your knitting.
- You can't be close to your markets while sitting in your office. The profit opportunities are in the field.

4

ROY'S RULE NO. 3:

Stay on Top of the Numbers

MAKING EXCEPTIONAL RESULTS HAPPEN

Owners make exceptional results happen by continually being on top of all the important numbers of their businesses, particularly the relationships that spell success, and the numbers that indicate real results. Relationships tell you how strong your company is financially. The key results numbers—working capital, costs, inventory and receivable turns, cash flow, gross margins and the like—tell you how you are going to make money. The important numbers have to be in your head at all times. They must be part of you, because they play a major role in every business decision you make.

What do you mean by "staying on top of the numbers," Roy?

As you know, I'm only interested in exceptional financial performance. Ordinary results? I'm not interested. The numbers of my business have a lot to do with getting me where I want to be. By "numbers," I'm talking about the relationships between the numbers, as well as the numerical results themselves. I'm always pushing myself to come up with numbers—results and relationships—that are better than anyone else's in my industry. For instance, if the norm in my industry for General and Administrative expense before I get paid is running over 15 percent of sales, I like to shoot for under 5 percent of sales because I know it's doable, and I know that performance will result in making me a lot of money. My numbers are not just some facts that are reported to me from time to time. To me, my company's numbers are alive. I keep trying to stay on top of them, all the time.

When you think about the numbers that really affect the success of your business, think about two types. First, you need to understand which numbers and relationships are critical to financial success in your industry. Some industry numbers may be pretty much out of anyone's control, such as the cost of power, so don't sweat those numbers. Other numbers and relationships, however, such as gross margin dollars in comparison with operating expenses, can make a tremendous difference in how profitable you can become, and how much cash you can take out of the business. These are the numbers to sweat over a lot, because knowledge of them can enable you to become financially successful and let you achieve your personal goals.

Second, it is equally important to stay on top of all the important numerical results and financial relationships of your own business at all times. With this information in hand, you will be in a position to compare actual company results with industry norms and your own financial and operational goals. This is a personal thing with me. I want to know what's happening in all the important performance areas if not daily, then at least weekly. I can't imagine independent business owners ever becoming solidly successful without constantly having their latest results numbers in their heads.

What's basic, then, to staying on top of the numbers?

It all starts with having a thorough and detailed knowledge of the basic financial relationships of your industry, relationships that create profits and cash flow. You need to have this basic knowledge in order to conceptualize how your company is going to make money, now and in the future. This knowledge has to drive everything owners do in deciding how to run their companies right.

If your volume, gross margins and operating expenses are in the right relationship to each other, you can make a tremendous amount of money in good economic times. And even during tough times, you can shrink in volume and still be profitable. Achieving this balance requires that you thoroughly understand the financial relationships that give you clues as to how you should run your business to make good profits and maintain continuous liquidity. These critical financial relationships include gross profit percentages, operating expense ratios, collection periods, and others, depending on your industry. You then need to develop a business strategy that will let you achieve extraordinary financial and operational results by taking concrete steps to deal successfully with these critical financial relationships. This is what making money is all about. I knew, for example, that if I could get my operating expense ratio well below 10 percent of sales, I could make a lot of money. Knowing in detail how you are going to do that and therefore make money is one of an owner's most fundamental responsibilities; to the company, and, of course, to the owner.

But don't get too carried away with "banker" numbers, including their favorite ratios—current ratio and debt to worth ratio. They are certainly important to your banker, but your obsession must be in running your company right in the first place. Sure, I look at the financial ratios of my business from time to time. But they're not what makes money for me. My first priority is to be totally on top of profits and positive cash flow, and all the things that affect them, *all the time*. If you are running your business right, the financial ratios will take care of themselves, and you will make good money.

You seem to have a special method for making money, Roy. Do you?

We're talking, of course, about running a regular, independent business. One that's managed by its owner. All the money in the business is the owner's, with maybe a little help from a credit line. We're not talking about an R & D-type company that is using other people's money to grow on—some genius who is coming up with super-conductivity in his garage. *When it's your company, every penny that heads in the wrong direction is cash out of your pocket.* Everything I do as an owner has a terrific impact on profits and cash, and therefore on making money and achieving my goals in life.

I find that everything today is very competitive. To be able to make a lot of money, I must have great products and great customers, but particularly I must have the lowest possible costs. That way I can take business from a position of strength. To be the lowest cost producer, I must have the lowest cost of money and the lowest selling expense. I also have to be the most productive outfit there is, totally. I have to work on improving my direct labor's productivity, and on minimizing the amount of fixed assets I need to support my direct labor. I need to know the level of gross margins my direct labor and its support can produce. And then, most importantly, I must make use of only the lowest possible level of overhead expense that will get the job done—putting great products into the hands of my great customers. There's just no reason to overkill *any* expense or investment. All my costs and investments must be no more than sufficient to support the mission of my company—being solidly successful at everything we do. That's how I make money. No big secrets there. It can work for you, too.

Are you getting that job done?

I work very hard at making sure I'm operating way above my breakeven sales volume so my cash flows are strongly positive. I have eliminated all nonessential General and Administrative costs. My G & A runs less than 4% of sales. People ask, "How do you do that?" There is a way to do it, and I'll be talking about that later. Depending on your industry, if you are currently at double-digit G & A, you probably need to take a hard look at all your business decisions. Something big must be wrong!

The sad truth is that most independent companies operate so close to their breakeven sales volume that they are vulnerable to the smallest glitch that comes along. If your business is in a mode where you have to do $11 million in sales just to break even, you should get out of that mode. *You absolutely must get out of that mode!* Get yourself into a mode where, even if you do $5 or $6 million in sales, everything is great. Don't get your costs to the point where you have to do big numbers just to break even. There will always be glitches. Life is full of glitches, and most of them are self-inflicted wounds. You'll be shooting yourself in the foot if your breakeven point is too high!

Just how critical is it, Roy, for an owner to be personally on top of the numbers?

What makes being on top of the numbers so critical? Listen. You own your business for the money it makes you and the life-style it affords you. You have to make a profit and generate cash or your business won't exist. Profits and cash flow are the results you are looking for. These results happen only if you are on top of the numbers. There is nothing more important to profitability and cash flow than getting to be on top of the numbers, and staying there. Owners need to concern themselves with three things: customers, products, and the numbers. Work all three right, and you will be profitable, and your cash flow will be positive. The profitability and cash flow of your company ultimately determine everything else. Profits and cash flow are power.

As with all important things in your business, you have to stay on top of the numbers yourself. An owner cannot delegate that job to anyone. Even if you have a controller, you still have to do it. In an independent business, you must be comfortable enough with the numbers that you are, in effect, your own Chief Financial Officer.

Besides profits and cash flow, owners need to think deeply about longevity. The ultimate measure of financial success is staying in business over a long period of time. I call that business "longevity," and that turns out to require continuous and predictable liquidity. Take your eyes off the numbers for very long, and you can kiss liquidity and longevity goodbye.

To be a solidly successful company, the charts of your business don't have to be a dramatic curve upwards that looks like Mt. Everest. They may not even be curves. They could be horizontal lines. They may just be chugging along a straight track. Whatever they are, the owner has to know what is happening with all the important numbers, all the time. That's how I make the numbers I'm trying to achieve happen. Don't ever be in the position of having the bank call you one fine morning and tell you they're calling in your credit line, and then sit there and wonder why this is happening to you and what you're going to do to save your rear end. If you want to stay in business for long, you'll need to watch the numbers a lot closer than that!

Sounds like that could take a lot of an owner's time. How on top of the numbers do you have to be, Roy?

Look. Your plan and goal is to transform products and services into cash profits. To do that, you have to rely on yourself to make the numbers work. Your staff can give you supporting data, but you must have a current sense of your financial situation at all times. What are the important numbers? For most businesses they are order rates, backlogs, shipments, gross profit, operating expenses, net profit, cash flows, working capital, receivables and receivables aging, inventory and inventory turns, and production rates.

These numbers need to be somewhere in your brain—your ready recall—at all times, because they are all so vital. You can't review graphs and other aids when you are six weeks down the road. It's too late then. You have to know the numbers *now.* That way, you know how to move forward, what orders to take, when to take them. It is something that just has to be within you, so you can depend totally on yourself when making important decisions. Most decisions you make have an impact on working capital. You can't tell how any decision will affect working capital unless you are totally on top of the numbers.

Of course, it helps if a company has a solid costing

system so the owner can accurately cost out present and future products, and get the information required to make decisions that will have as positive an impact on working capital as possible. Today, excellent costing systems are available with a minimal investment in computers and software. You have to be able to get at accurate costs quickly, and you have to feel secure about your costing. If you are able to factor in all elements of cost in making any business decision—everything that has any impact at all on being profitable and staying liquid, you have a much better chance of becoming and remaining solidly successful.

How about the other important numbers?

You should know your cash position and your actual operating and direct costs and expenditures daily, or at least weekly, so you can compare the real world with the cash flow projections you must make to help you predict your future cash position. You need this information so you can take immediate action if costs are getting out of line or your cash balance is dwindling.

Owners of smaller businesses simply cannot afford surprises when it comes to cash and costs. Your operations, whatever they may be, must produce only profitable business that adds to positive cash flow. If anything is causing you to deviate from that goal, you must get on top of it immediately, and correct the problem. The woods are full of failed companies that didn't know they were in cash-trouble or cost-trouble until it was too late.

In addition, owners should receive regular management reports that cover all key performance indicators on a regular basis, but no less frequently than weekly. You need to determine what the key results indicators are for your business, and then make sure you can see those numbers weekly or more frequently. Monthly reports, such as normal financial statements, are important, but they don't give you the information you need to be really on top of the numbers. Make sure that any weekly reports you do get are simple in format and easy to understand.

You need to talk about your key performance numbers continually—at least weekly—with your management team. Do this faithfully, no matter where you may be, even if you are off on vacation enjoying the fruits of your company's performance. Doing so keeps your management group working towards commonly understood goals. It also helps you determine where you must improve performance to stay on track with your expectations.

How does knowing the numbers help the owner deal with customers?

Having a complete knowledge of the numbers is absolutely critical when negotiating a contract with a customer. To negotiate from strength, you have to know all your financial parameters, especially your gross margins and where your General and Administrative and other overhead costs are running. It's not all that difficult, but you have to know those things. Just as important to you is knowing that you can produce the goods very close to what your costing tells you they should cost. You should also know that, due to the lean and mean way you are operating, no one can make the product for less, unless there is something going on that isn't cricket, like a competitor selling for less than cost. This gives you the power to close orders that are going to be profitable.

Profits are important, but you also need to look at the cash requirements of the deal; the terms, the inventory turns, the cash flow from collections. You just have to be constantly aware of all of this, because *working capital runs your business, just as it runs my business*. You may have a customer and a great product, but it takes cash and working capital to make all that gel together into a good bottom line and on-going liquidity.

Roy, this sounds very complicated. Shouldn't an owner get outside financial help?

I know many owners who get outside help to collect the numbers and even to interpret the numbers. They sign up financial advisors and accounting firms to do much of the internal accounting, including monthly financial statements and even cost accounting. I feel an owner is better served by generating those numbers in-house. You get to see the numbers more rapidly, and you can keep your "professional services" costs down. Having done that, you can then have your numbers reviewed by a CPA firm, quarterly or annually, if necessary.

Most owners I know get outside help for their quarterly financial statements. I use my accounting firm only for an annual review. The less an outside accounting firm does for you, and the more you can track internally, the better off you will be in making business decisions, provided your numbers are correct. That's one way to make sure the owner stays on top of the numbers.

Did you ever let the numbers get away from you?

Not really, but I came awfully close recently. I took some business that I knew would squeeze my working capital. So I took special steps to make sure I could get through the tight period. Fortunately, I got through it by being on top of the numbers, but I don't recommend the heartburn that resulted to anyone!

As it happened, I took an extra-large amount of early-year business because times had been tough. I wanted to make sure that my total year was going to be a good one. After I took on a large, new customer, I found that the new account could only pay me in 50 days, instead of the normal 30. This big customer was going to extend my total receivables from 28 to 40 days. That was a formula for a cash crunch if there ever was one. This uncomfortable situation forced me to dip into my credit line. Fortunately, my credit line drawdown was at zero. I have a great relationship with my bank. On second thought, I'm not sure *anyone* has a great relationship with a bank. I have a great relationship with my *wife!* No other relationship comes close! Back to business . . . Because I wanted to maintain my great relationship with my bank, I did my cash flow projections two or three times. It seemed like it was a safe risk to take.

I knew the worst-case scenario if I were to take the order. It was a gamble, but I knew the numbers. At worst, I would only make a small profit on the job this season. At best, I would make out very well, especially in future years. Besides, I wanted to do it and make it work. The order fit exactly within the framework of how I wanted to develop my business.

I gave some thought to financing the order based on my personal assets. I firmly believe, however, that a business should stand on its own. Owners shouldn't have to dip into their own assets to run their business. That doesn't mean I wouldn't use my personal assets in the business in an emergency. But, if you have a personal cushion somewhere in your life, keep it. Hold onto it. Everybody needs a little cushion somewhere. Cushions are meant *not* to be used.

It was important to me to take care of this particular cash crunch problem without using my personal assets. So I got the bank to increase my line of credit. If I were to take this order, I knew it was not a crazy flier. I was confident it was doable, but I also knew that it would stretch me.

When the buyer and I talked about the order, I said, in my entrepreneurial spirit, "I think I can do that." But after our meeting, I went back to the hotel room and thought about the order, and gave the numbers another look. It was very close. Not much gross margin. I reviewed it with my plant manager by phone, and went over the costing again. I wanted to review everything because it was going to be so very tight.

The next day I went back to the customer and took the order. They were gracious, and offered me part of it, but I was greedy and took it all. I seized the opportunity! The order was worth several hundred thousand dollars, and it was going to put me in a position to make this product for the next five to ten years. It's a temptation, sometimes, to take business that maybe I shouldn't.

You can probably guess what happened. Owners can always count on having production glitches somewhere along the line when they take on new customers and increase their business. That's a given, and it caught up with me. I had a major production glitch with this order. Also, I wasn't really certain how easy it was going to be to collect this receivable on time. In this case, the receivable turned out to be of the slow-pay variety. I had these two things working against me, but I was aware of the possibilities and had factored these potential problems into my cash plans. Both problems worked against me. The result was, of course, that I got strung out on cash. I had to go to the maximum of my working capital line of credit in a great, big hurry.

Months after I took this order, it was still being produced. I just had to perform for this important customer. I said I could do it, so I was committed. As James Bond says, "Your word is your bond." This was an effort, basically, to break into a new customer. The risks were there, but I felt my company could deal with them.

It all worked out in our favor, but I would never have gambled that way if I hadn't been totally on top of—and ahead of—the numbers.

Then being on top of the numbers saved your goose?

The point is that I really stretched myself to develop a new customer that could lead to good things for my company in the future. It ended up stretching my cash position. I even had to line up a new bank. When the crunch came, we got through it by the skin of our teeth. I was glad when it was over, but I would do it all over again because *I was on top of the numbers.* I knew I could make it work.

Isn't that a lot of the fun of business, stretching yourself and taking reasonable risks to make a customer happy? In this case, I won the gamble. The customer is happy, and I'm very happy.

The Quick-Study Guide
for Independent Business Owners

STAY ON TOP OF THE NUMBERS

- Know the financial relationships that assure high cash profits in your industry, and then make them happen in your company.
- Review all the key performance numbers frequently. Make them part of you—in your brain, in your ready recall.
- Be your own "Chief Financial Officer." Work the numbers for profitability, cash flow, and for the ultimate goal—business longevity.
- Knowledge of the key numbers is essential when negotiating with customers.
- If you are operating near breakeven sales volume, get out of that mode, fast!
- Do most of the numbers crunching internally, using your own people. The numbers will be more understandable and meaningful to you, and you will be more on top of them.
- Review the key performance-indicator numbers weekly, or even daily.
- Continuously communicate the key operations numbers with your management team.
- Don't take on a "stretch" project or program unless you are totally on top of the numbers and comfortable that you can make them work for you.

5

ROY'S RULE NO. 4:

Hammer Overhead

ELIMINATING NON-ESSENTIAL COSTS

Allow only those overhead expenses that are absolutely required to get the job done—*and no more.* You
only make money from direct labor. All other expenses are
just so much excess baggage, and must be minimized or
eliminated. This applies to all operating expenses, including management team and staff personnel. For maximum
profits, fight non-productive overhead costs every inch of
the way. It's much easier to disallow a new expense than
to get rid of an entrenched expense.

---

*These days, everybody is down-sizing,
right-sizing, getting lean and mean—as
you say, "Hammering Overhead."
What's different about your approach?*

I determined when I started my company that if I was
going to succeed the way I wanted to succeed, Southwest
Apparel had to be the lowest cost producer in its business.
So, I started with the thinnest cost structure anyone could
imagine, determined to run a highly efficient company. I
have never departed from that philosophy. I don't need

to downsize like most of my competitors are doing because my overhead never had a chance to grow. I'm not talking about putting on the green eye shades and nitpicking, or just being cheap. I know where I have to spend money—like making my production workers highly productive, treating them right, and turning out a great, quality product that my customers really love. Will I spend money for anything that doesn't contribute to that? *No way! I'm not interested!*

My overall philosophy is that I need to run the most efficient, lowest overhead operation possible in my industry. Everybody talks about doing that; few succeed. They get side-tracked along the way with great sounding stuff that simply adds to overhead. Like signing up for expensive outside services when you'd be better off doing it yourself—with your existing staff. Don't let that crap sneak up on you!

Of course, the owner has to set the tone. I control all the company's cash, coming in and going out. So I control where we spend every cent. I continually review where we are thinking of spending money, whether it is an expense item or an investment of some type. It's all cash to me. If it goes to anything that doesn't make money for me, I lose. I don't like to lose.

In addition, I've got everybody in the company thinking and living "savings." Almost everything you buy these days is a commodity. Whatever it is, you can buy it somewhere for less. And there are better times to buy things than other times. Everybody in the company understands that our intent is to get the most out of every dollar we spend, whether it's for people, services, materials or things—like office supplies. We take advantage of every opportunity to save. That's a philosophy every owner should drill into every employee. I tell our people, "Let's save $200 a year on this and spend it on a company picnic. Let's save $2,000 here and $20,000 there, and then we'll be able to buy that great piece of production equipment." They all get the message.

Making money and not spending money are two different things, aren't they, Roy?

There's no good reason these days for a smaller, independent company not to have the lowest overhead cost structure possible in its industry. By "overhead" costs, I'm thinking about every single cash output that is not directly involved in making and shipping my products, including money spent on management and staff, fancy facilities, or operating expenses. I learned early on that I *only* make money in my manufacturing business by applying direct labor to production. Everything else is just so much excess baggage.

Of course, all owners need to make their direct labor as productive as possible. But I don't waste money on things that are not productive, and neither should you. This applies across the board. It never made any sense to me to put a big effort into making my factory efficient, and then have a bloated headquarters staff. You can't hammer overhead out in the factory, and then go through Door A into the office area only to find a bunch of staff people drinking coffee and playing with their computer screens. When you commit to saving money everywhere you possibly can, you have to be consistent. There can be no exceptions. Keep looking for overhead expense reductions—everywhere!

The difference between the normal "ho-hum" company and an exceptionally profitable one usually shows up in how well each company controls overhead. Smart owners fight like hell before any new expenses are added. In most businesses, the marketplace determines what your percentage gross margin can be, within a few points. You can try reducing materials and other direct costs all you want, but the big difference in profitability usually shows up in overhead as a percent of sales. Say the best companies in your industry are experiencing 35% gross margins, and you are within a few points of that. But also say the best companies are spending about 22% of sales on General and Administrative expenses before owner withdrawals. What's to keep you from spending only 6% on the same stuff? Instead of the 13% net income before owner withdrawals that the "best" are doing, you earn 29% before withdrawals and taxes. Not a bad deal.

You're wondering what hammering overhead would do for your company? I'll tell you what hammering overhead can do. First, it puts your business in a favorable position competitively. No one can push you around. You're the cost king. Second, when times get tough and volume falls off, you have a great big safety cushion that helps you stay alive and profitable even in the worst of times. Finally, guess who gets to earn a terrific return on investment? You! That's what it's all about.

To prevent needless spending, put a great big hurdle in front of every wonderful idea for spending money. Nip it in the bud, and look for ways to accomplish the objective without spending new money. It's one heck of a lot easier to stop a new expense before it starts than later when you are forced to cut back.

Cutting expenses is much tougher than stopping expenses. Profits come from keeping focused on applying direct labor to filling orders. That's where you make money. All other expenses are just a drag.

Aren't people costs your largest overhead item?

People expenses are usually the largest share of

operating expenses for most independent businesses, and management salaries can be the largest share of that. These days, owners simply cannot afford to have large management staffs, or their cost structures will throw them out of the ballpark in the world economy, or even in the local economy. I've kept the total bill for my company's management and staff costs low from the start. We've only had on board the minimum complement of people necessary to get the job done. It has made a huge difference. I see the difference this makes everyday in my bank account's balance.

When starting a new company, or when you are reviewing where you are, it is absolutely essential that you commit to operating with the minimum number of managers. Look at all the basic functions that are essential to your business, and then work on getting them done them with as few managers and support personnel as possible. Forget about tightly-defined job descriptions. That's a sure prescription for excessive overhead. I assign crossover duties to every manager. My managers are well-paid, so I have no qualms asking every manager, including myself, to do multiple tasks. Everybody becomes more productive, including me. You can always add someone when an extra person is needed, but it's very difficult to eliminate surplus people. If you start with the minimum complement of managers in the first place, you will end up with a tight, well-run management team.

As I said before, I take care of all our "externals" myself. I'm my own chief salesman, chief marketeer, chief financial officer, chief negotiator with the bank, even chief buyer for piece goods. Nevertheless, I can't do everything. I need an exceptional operations manager to run my production plants in Tennessee so I can handle my owner responsibilities well—working the "externals." I'm fortunate. My operations manager is the best!

How do I get and keep efficient and productive people like my operations manager; people who will do anything, who have no inhibitions about work, who are completely self-reliant? It helps, in fact, to find someone with a small town up-bringing, one who doesn't mind getting grease under his or her fingernails, and even prefers it.

Still, the example of self-reliance has to come from the owner. Managers have to see that the owner is willing and able to do anything. I'll do anything! I'll make a plane reservation, I'll go stand in line, I'll pack a carton and get it shipped. Whatever it takes! I have no secretary or even an office. My office is in my home. It would cost at least $75,000 a year to have an office in Phoenix with an "assistant." Who needs that? I'd rather have the $75,000 in my bank account!

The entire management staff of my $5 million manufacturing company consists of myself, the operations manager, an administrator, and eight line supervisors. That's it. That's how you get an extremely productive management staff. I set the example. I show them they can do anything it takes to get the job done, as long as it's legal and moral, and as long as they don't add nonproductive people.

As I see it, having too many managers creates overlapping responsibilities, confusion, and unproductive use of management talent. Owners of small, independent businesses just can't allow any part of their businesses to be inefficient. And besides, with a thin management staff, the owner can structure a pay-for-performance plan so the few managers you do have can make more money. That really helps everyone's motivation and *esprit de corps*.

It doesn't make sense to pay exorbitant salaries for managers, or anyone else, for that matter. The larger companies in the apparel industry typically pay well into six figures for operations and financial managers. No wonder they are hurting! No wonder more and more apparel sold in the United States is manufactured overseas. Of course, owners need to pay fair value for services rendered, and include some interesting incentives. But they just don't need to pay exorbitant salaries, especially if they stay away from operating in high-cost regions of the country. People often ask me about the benefits we provide our employees, like fully company-paid health insurance, paid vacations, or paid sick leave. I could put a whole basket of benefits together for my employees and go broke. I believe in paying well for performance. Most smaller companies just can't go the complete benefits-basket route and compete, let alone survive. *The benefit I pay is cash.* My workers are paid very well, but, better yet, they get to keep their jobs, because we work hard at keeping employment level *by being competitive in the global economy.* The way I look at it, that's a benefits package worth having!

You have a small headquarters staff that helps your managers be more efficient, don't you, Roy?

Hell, no! One of the great things about being a smaller company is that there's no real need for a staff of non-productive people supposedly helping management do their managing and decision-making. Let the big companies suffer along with overstaffing. I don't need a staff, and I'll bet you don't, either.

At Southwest Apparel, we don't have *any* staff people of the non-productive type. Everyone produces something. Even our plant administrator doubles as payroll clerk, bookkeeper, purchasing agent, computer jockey and receptionist. Everyone has tasks that directly relate to selling, making and shipping great products. No unproductive staff people making work for each other and the managers. Our managers are paid to make decisions themselves. They support themselves.

Since our management team is so small, it is very close-knit. I talk to my operations manager at least once every day. He talks to his general supervisor and the line supervisors many times a day. We all know what we are trying to get done. No one is confused about the operations plan. Since we communicate so well together, we have no need for formal staff meetings or written plans. This eliminates any need for a staff of "helpers." And, in my opinion, this is where solid success begins. This allows a company to make money. *No unproductive staff people, got it?*

Our small management team eliminates the need for staff people in several ways. We make extensive use of our simple personal computer system, not only for doing all of our accounting and payroll record-keeping, but also to help us in our production processes. Companies our size don't need expensive mid-range computers. We get along just fine with an inexpensive personal computer. Powerful, low-cost software is available these days. The personal computer enables us to eliminate the need for an entire accounting department. Some payback!

It's also not beneath us to take advantage of the support services provided by our vendors. They do a great job on such things as fabric design, and we are happy to let them do that for us. I don't think owners should get hung up on trying to do everything themselves. If there are outsiders who can do some things for you for free, or cheaper than you could do it with an internal staff, accept their assistance. The staff people you might have added would probably have been under-employed part of the time. Don't be proud. Don't hire them in the first place.

Work loads go up and down. Everything in life goes up and down. Someone gets a little stretched, and right away, the tendency is to add another person. As soon as you bring someone on board, another employee gets unstretched, and you're stuck with an extra employee only half busy. What you really needed was half a person, but they're hard to come by.

If someone gets too stretched out to handle the load, we try to have someone fill in on a part-time basis, preferably someone from the factory. This happens now and again when we are complying with the paperwork required by government regulations. No way am I going to add full-time people to do that kind of unproductive work. We get it done, one way or the other, with our existing, lean staff, and no one gets stretched out of shape.

I also make a big thing about having few written operational reports and plans; better yet, none. Such reports can be killers on overhead expense, no matter how well-intentioned they may be. People keep telling me we need a marketing plan or maybe better yet a strategic plan. *BS!* I am the plan. We are the plan. Forget all that "business plan" crap. It doesn't earn you a cent. This is one of the benefits of owning a small company. You, the owner, can be out in the marketplace, and at the same time run an efficient, low-overhead business, turning out a great product or service. *That way, you and your company are the plan!*

I'm convinced that this area alone, keeping non-productive staff people to an absolute minimum—*meaning none*—accounts for the largest part of my low cost structure. Keep that in mind. It's tempting to add staff support people. Just don't do it.

What other operating expenses do you hammer, Roy?

Beyond people costs, the most obvious area to look at is facilities. They are really visible to everyone, and they send a message about an owner's priorities to managers and employees, and even to customers and suppliers. In case you haven't noticed, glitz is out. If your facilities are glitzy, the message you are putting out is, "We really care about appearances, not results." Worse yet, your customers may start thinking they are overpaying to maintain excessive overhead. It makes absolutely no sense in today's competitive and economic climate to have facilities that are overly fancy or too spacious.

I'm talking about manufacturers, of course, so I suppose you could make an argument that fancy offices help sell, say, your advertising agency services. Maybe so, but I don't think so. That kind of thinking went out in the late 1980s when we woke up to the realities of global competition. Now, "plain-pipe-racks" is in. Low cost is in. Making money is in. Surviving in tough times is in. I know more owners who got stuck with fancy, excessively large facilities during the 1980s, and now they're trying desperately to get out of them and into something that makes economic sense.

If a business is not a well-oiled, efficient machine, everything can get out of sync when some area isn't pulling its weight. In order to be successful today, everything must be operating at capacity or overcapacity. I'm talking about people and facilities. They both need to be a little overused.

Next to payroll, our biggest expense is rent for our factory buildings. I have no intention of ever owning any of our production facilities. That would significantly reduce my flexibility for future developments. Besides, there are some great deals these days on short-term leases for factory and office space. The rent for both our factory buildings is extremely low. I intend to keep it that way. I can't imagine why a company would have it any other way.

When I see factory offices where there is a lot of unused space, I can smell that something is wrong. Factory offices should be next to the production floor.

Why would an owner want them anyplace else? Look at Mars Candy. They are famous for running efficient operations. Their factory offices are right next to the production lines, where they can see the M & M's popping out. That's where my factory offices are—at the factory. I believe office space needs to be kept dense—full. Busy, all the time. Everybody elbow-to-elbow. If you saw my Tennessee plant offices, you'd know what I mean. I haven't rented space for "growth." We only rent space for "current." It's just common sense. You can always add on if necessary, or get a little space somewhere nearby. Stay lean on space.

Of course, there are certain essential operating expenses, and I'm all for them, as long as they are not excessive. But there are also *nonessential* operating expenses. I am continually looking for them, so I can hammer them. No one is going to squander expenses but me—which means we aren't going to squander anything.

To minimize our phone bill, for instance, the administrator uses the 800 numbers of our suppliers and even customers whenever possible. The factory's phone bill, as a result, is less than mine. The factory talks on the phone as much or more than I do, but the administrator is religious about using 800 numbers whenever possible. We even decided to keep personal phone call expense down by installing a pay phone in the plant.

We are always looking for trucking firms that offer better rates for freight. We compare freight rates and try different trucking firms to get the best combination of service and price. We monitor these costs month to month.

All of the operating expenses that I've been talking about can add up fast if you're not on top of them. By hammering overhead, pretty soon the savings add up to big money, right there on your bottom line!

What you're saying about hammering overhead sounds so obvious. Doesn't just about every independent business owner control expenses the same way?

You've gotta be kidding! In my experience, very few business owners pay nearly enough attention to operating costs. A few years ago, I was visiting an old friend of mine in Chicago. Bill and I had worked together at Union Carbide back in the 1960s, where we both were salesmen. We had gone our separate ways, and Bill eventually bought a small household goods manufacturing company which he had grown to about $15 million in sales. He told me over the phone that he had two manufacturing plants, one on the south side of Chicago and the other in a small town in Arkansas. He also said he couldn't wait to show me around his new offices near O'Hare Airport. Since I was coming through town, we just had to get together for old times sake.

Of course, I was a bit suspicious from the start. What is a $15 million manufacturer doing with "new offices" near O'Hare in a fancy office park. Who knows? Here I go.

Just as I imagined, the office complex looked fantastic—and expensive. The reception area fit the scene. Fancy wood. Pricey paintings and furniture. And then, best of all—the receptionist. She was good-looking, of course, but damned if she didn't have a wonderful English accent. We all lived through the era of the 1980s when it was in vogue to have an English-accented receptionist. That was a big deal. A receptionist from England, or maybe from Australia—most Americans couldn't tell the difference. English-accented receptionists commanded more money than just your typical, ordinary American-accented receptionist.

I'll never forget her name. Eileen Throckmorton. Eileen was a delight. She told me that Bill was just finishing a staff meeting, and would be out to greet me in a few minutes. She said, "May I offer you some tea?" Unbelievable!

So I picked up a magazine, trying to look busy, but my eyes couldn't help wandering. To the great-looking English receptionist, of course, but also beyond her, down the hall to the office area. I noticed more of those fancy paintings on the walls—coordinated, of course. I could also plainly see a number of people wandering around, wearing white shirts and ties. I got the impression these were staff people of some sort. They looked like they had never seen the insides of a factory.

Bill's meeting went on and on, so I had time to lapse off into a reverie. The contrast between all this and my own factory offices in central Tennessee was just too much. We do have a tiny reception area where a visitor can sit down, but that's where the similarity ends. Our receptionist is also the administrator. As I said, she is a very busy lady. She does many things. You'll be lucky to get her attention at all when you walk in, let alone get offered tea. Not that she is rude. She's just busy. We're lean and mean, remember?

And then, look at our factory offices. Plain, simple, crowded, and right next to the factory floor. No glitz. Everybody with work clothes on. There to work! No staff people at all, like Bill had.

Then I had a wild thought. I'll bet that Bill is worried about his costs, and is about to go to the other extreme. You know, get a voice mail system to replace this high-priced English receptionist. He probably thinks he should go from this beautiful, $25,000 per year, English-accented receptionist, to a $20,000 per year voice mail set up.

That kind of thinking drives me crazy. He should be considering a happy, $12,000 per year employee with a nice telephone voice working down at the factory and handling everything—not just being a receptionist. That would save a hell of a lot more money. Of course, I'm prejudiced against voice mail. Wastes too much of my time, and time is money.

So, here I am, selling $5 million of cheap shorts and making good money, and there's Bill, selling $15 million of household goods, with all these people helping him. I could see that it was going to be interesting, hearing how well he was doing.

Enough of this idle reverie! Into the fancy reception area bursts Bill, greeting me like the old friends that we were. "How the hell are you, Roy. You look great. Boy, am I glad to see you! I've got a lot of things to talk to you about."

I knew I was in for a long afternoon.

So what did you and Bill talk about, Roy, that was so important to your friend?

Just guess what we talked about! About how he grew his company from $5 million to $15 million really fast. How he was making less money now than when he was a $5 million business. How, in spite of everything he tried, he couldn't keep his costs in line. How he wished he wasn't stuck with those long-term leases. How he was operating at break-even and the bank was getting damned nervous.

Guess why he needed to talk about these things? Only one reason. *Bill hadn't been hammering overhead . . . all the time!*

The Quick-Study Guide for Independent Business Owners

HAMMER OVERHEAD

• Keep hammering overhead, *all the time.*
• Avoid having to downsize by not adding excessive management and staff in the first place.
• Having productive managers starts at the top—with you.
• Small companies should be able to get along just fine with a very small headquarters support staff, preferably none.
• There's no need whatsoever to pay exorbitant manager salaries. Pay for value, not for show.
• Add-on tasks to existing employees before adding people.
• Cutting expenses is much tougher than stopping expenses before they start.
• Get everyone to live "savings" and "efficiency."
• You only make money on direct labor that is working to fill orders. All other expenses are just costs to be avoided wherever possible.
• Minimize costs *everywhere.* Be consistently tough on all elements of cost.
• Whatever it is that you are buying, you can probably buy it cheaper if you shop around.
• With facilities, glitz is out; "plain-pipe-racks" is in. Overextend the use of all facilities and people before even thinking about adding anything or anyone.

6

ROY'S RULE NO. 5:

Simplify! Simplify! Simplify!

AVOIDING COSTLY COMPLEXITIES

If you're going to own the most productive operation around, you simply must avoid unnecessary complexity. Running a highly successful, small, independent business is not all that tough if you keep everything simple. Complexity breeds costs—costs that cannot be permitted for maximum productivity, profitability and cash flow.

Why are you so hung up on simplicity, Roy?

Running a highly successful, independent business isn't all that tough. But if owners let things get complex, costs get out of line and they'll lose one of their biggest competitive advantages. By keeping all processes and practices as simple and easily understood as they possibly can be, owners can keep hidden costs low or nonexistent, and that will help maximize productivity, profitability and cash flow.

I try to keep my eyes on my customers continuously,

concentrating on what I have to do to satisfy them totally and make them want to come back for more. The processes to accomplish this most fundamental of business aims must be simple and direct. I work hard to keep it that way.

As a manufacturer, I keep in mind that all I'm trying to do is get my products from the shop to the ultimate end user, with a happy retailer in between. The company that does the best job of that wins. A winning company makes life simple for itself.

People lose sight of the basics of making money, because most business people have a natural tendency to over-organize things. They are busy complicating the mission of business, which is to create a great product or service, bring it to the marketplace, sell it to satisfied and happy customers, and get paid for it. That's the mission. All that other "stuff" is just "stuff."

Roy, how should smaller businesses implement simple practices and processes?

All good things in business are not necessarily cheap, but they sure ought to be simple. To run efficiently, a business operation doesn't have to be all that tough or complicated. Large corporations have a real disadvantage compared to independent businesses. They usually have such large, complex, "professional" organizations that they must use the old Army rule, "Put everything in writing." That procedure explains why so many large companies have such high overheads, with obscenely large staffs pushing paper every which way. Smaller businesses can get the job done without most of the over-organized complexities of large companies. Because they are small, everybody is close to the action. That makes running them simpler.

The "experts" tell us a tremendous amount of information is needed to run a business. They make it sound so complicated. But by looking behind the scenes and figuring out what you really need to know and do, it just isn't all that complicated. Owners can keep it simple, because it is simple. This isn't rocket-scientist stuff. It's easy. Parting the Red Sea was hard. Running a solid, simple business isn't.

To keep your business simple, you and your people have to stay really focused on the present and the immediate future—the *now*. If you can't resist planning ahead, you can speculate on what might be happening down the road by developing a five-year plan, but you should know it won't be worth a damn to you. There are only a few immediate things that you and your people have to stay focused on—products, customers, backlog, overhead, profitability and cash flow. If you do that, you'll succeed. If you don't, you're going to miss the boat.

I'm always amused when I see the financial statements of a smaller business that take a "Ph.D.-CPA"—not just an ordinary CPA—to figure out what's going on. I started my business in an era when there was a trend for businesses to have four or five different companies to cover all the inside deals. The family owned the equipment, they leased it back to the company, etc. Typically, if a company did $10 million, their financial statements were at least fifteen pages long. There were numerous footnotes and all that crap. The company structure was so complicated, I wondered how they got anything done right, or how they knew what was really going on with the business. Owners who want to understand things and be on top of their businesses should just try to keep everything as simple as possible, including their financial statements.

This philosophy carries through just about everything we do at Southwest Apparel. The sales reporting, the manufacturing processes, the materials ordering process—every practice that we use. The trouble with allowing things to get overly complicated is that *complications breed costs,* and *complications tend to multiply.* If you're trying to be lean and mean, you just can't burden yourself with unnecessary processes or duties. Concentrate on what counts. Forget the rest.

What role should the owner play, Roy, in keeping things uncomplicated?

I go out of my way to keep things from becoming complicated. I don't care if it's the way we put something in a carton, or how we take an order. Life is pretty basic, beautiful and simple, and success can also be simple. But the owner really has to work at it all the time, or complexity will slowly creep into the operation. When it does, the owner is going to have a much tougher job making money.

You're the owner! Don't allow yourself or your management team to get bogged down in what I call "professional management" tasks. Don't assign a new person to every task that some "expert" recommends. This is the fundamental reason why so many companies are being forced to downsize their administrative staffs— they're loaded down with overlapping flab. You need to find alternatives—ways to satisfy these so-called "needs" through suppliers or outside support organizations, or better yet, by using existing, already "fully-loaded" personnel. Assign "additional duties" to your existing staff. You can bet they'll find the simplest way to set priorities and get their additional duties done fast.

A big danger is to bring in advisors to help you do your job. Advisors tend to complicate things, because that's their business. All of a sudden, you're talked into commissioning an expensive study. Then you get a chance to read a voluminous report that says you've been doing it wrong all this time. Give me a break! Figure it out yourself. It's not all that tough!

Roy, how do you keep your management and organizational structure from becoming complicated?

A cardinal rule for keeping everything simple is to *have a very small, tightly knit management team, then keep the verbal communication going throughout the team, constantly.* I never have formal meetings with all of my managers, because I talk with most of them individually almost every day on the phone. We all know which new orders are coming down the pike, how well production is filling existing orders, and where we sit on cash. There's no need to write these conversations down. We all know what's happening—all the time.

The fewer written rules you have, the better. We write down as few policy and procedure proclamations as possible. We do have some basic personnel rules covering areas that some workers might abuse, such as not smoking on the line, or not staying in the john too long. We write down these few personnel policies and put them on the employees' bulletin board. But we make our policies known to all employees verbally and continuously, through the chain of command. Our supervisors meets with each operator once a month to discuss subjects of mutual interest, including reinforcing the personnel rules. This practice is not only less work than drafting formal pronouncements, but it's really effective at getting all employees to understand and comply.

As far as running the company is concerned, *I don't want to have any epistles, like five-year strategic plans, sitting on the shelf and gathering dust.* Life and business are living things. Change is constant. My whole management team participates in running the show. Since the

show is always changing, we find that having frequent
verbal conversations among the key players keeps everybody heading in the right direction. It saves lots of
complications.

What are some other key areas to work on in keeping everything simple and direct?

Southwest Apparel is a small firm. We can't afford to
become over-proceduralized. We want to produce qual
ity products, but we also want to keep everything simple.
I keep studying every process and practice that we use to
run the company, looking for ways to simplify our
methods and improve results.

For instance, we publish the performance of every
operator, every day. All operators know immediately
what is really important for them to know. We now use
a simple, computerized, performance reporting system to
do this. They see their performance on a piece of paper,
as well as that of their line mates. We also have an in-line
quality system that reports on quality problems as soon as
they occur. If there are quality problems, we want to
know about them right away, so we can fix them immediately. Our simple reports keep our factory people
really focused on the most important things for them—
production, productivity and quality.

Frankly, I was surprised to find out how using the
latest computer technology can streamline internal operations and keep everybody informed. As I have said,
we have been able to eliminate the need for an entire
accounting department by the use of our simple computer system. We seem to be finding new computer
applications all the time that get some part of the whole
job done better, faster, and with fewer complications.

Another example of simplicity at work is the management reports sent to me every week by the factory. I only get four management reports. These reports, along with daily conversations with my management team, give me the information I need to be totally on top of what is going on. They also tell me what we need to do to improve results. The management reports I get weekly are a cash requirements projection that spells out what we owe every week for about two months, an open accounts receivables report, a shipping report, and an operations report. These reports are all I need to stay on top of results.

My "corporate" office is in my home. I keep no files, and have no secretary. When I'm in my office, I'm on the phone most of the day, talking to customers, our reps and the factory. These conversations drive my company without the need for the reports, letters and paperwork that clutter up many owners' in-boxes.

My first job was as a sales correspondent for a large company. I wrote endless letters, just as my boss told me to write them. After doing that for eight months, I realized how futile and non-productive the job was. Maybe that's why I'm totally against all of the letter-writing that consumes so much of a chief executive's time. I have a nice, simple pad of note paper with my name printed on it. I only send hand-written notes, if I write anybody at all. These notes go to customers; to anyone. I usually print them, and I make them right to the point. I avoid all the flowery language. Everybody seems to appreciate the directness of my simple correspondence. I save a lot of money by not having a secretary, and by not being in the letter-writing business.

Of course, how we produce our apparel, how we order materials, how we take and ship orders, and how we make collections are vital to any garment manufacturer, so we put a big effort into making these processes work smoothly and efficiently. All operations can always be done better, so we're constantly working on ways to improve them.

Like most companies, we have to deal with the reporting requirements of government agencies—OSHA, EPA, IRS, et al. Other companies hire people just to do this work. I don't know why. We don't. I'm not going to hire a staff to do this work—no way! I'm just not going to pay a wage to anyone who is not directly productive. I manage to get my compliance work done through my existing employees. Somebody does it, and that some-body is already on the payroll. Sometimes I fill out reports myself. If we're not sure how to fill them out, we call someone and find out. No big deal. Don't let these reports complicate your business, or before you know it, you'll have a whole department just to do compliance work. I just won't allow it to happen! You shouldn't, either.

Roy, please give me an example of simplicity in action.

I have always tried hard to keep my annual financial statements extremely simple. I try to make them under-standable, almost to the point where some people ques-tion their believability. I originally thought I was doing this to make life easy for anyone who had a need to understand my business, completely and quickly. As it turned out, however, there was a direct financial payback from making my financial statements simple.

When I first started the company and was building the business, I made it a point to clear up my credit line at year-end, which, of course, helps simplify my year-end statements. I know everyone can't do that, but it works for me. Banks like to see any company get out of their line of credit at least once a year.

As it turned out, I wasn't able to zero it out one year recently. All of a sudden, things started getting more complicated. We had to ask ourselves, how do we handle this? Is it long-term or short-term debt? When did the checks go to the computer? When were they actually mailed out? Do we need to reclassify our receivables? Accounting problems sprang up that we didn't have before.

As a result, I had many more conversations with my accounting firm than usual. Instead of one $1,000 meeting with the accounting firm, I was stuck with three meetings. Life became a lot more complicated for me, just because I hadn't stuck to my plan to have simple financial statements that reflect a zero balance on the credit line at year's end.

The point of the story is that I had always kept my financial reporting simple up to that point. I never had statement-closing problems before. I had created a discipline for the company to have the simplest, most easily understood statements in the world. Something a dummy could understand. One year I made it a little more complicated and it cost me a lot. Never again. Now we do it the simple way.

So simplicity really pays off for you, Roy?

We all know how complicated life can get. Business owners have to fight the tendency to make their businesses more complicated than they need to be. Often, the easiest way out of a problem is to come up with a complicated solution. The simple, direct, low-overhead solutions may take a little more thought and work to figure out. But that's your job as owner—to keep looking for simpler ways to get the work of your company done right.

If you allow complications to work their insidious way into your business operations and practices, it will be impossible for your company to have the lowest cost structure in your industry. By keeping *everything* simple and direct, you can build a productive, profitable and solidly successful company.

The Quick-Study Guide for Independent Business Owners

SIMPLIFY! SIMPLIFY! SIMPLIFY!

• Complications increase costs. Complications tend to multiply.

• Don't allow your people to get bogged down with purely "professional management" or government-regulation compliance tasks. Assign "additional duties" to existing personnel. Make *everyone* a direct producer.

• Have a small, tightly knit management team, that verbally communicates together frequently. This reduces communications problems and helps promote simplicity.

• The fewer written rules, the better.

• Keep studying your operating practices, looking for simpler and better ways to get the job done. Fight the tendency to make your business more complicated.

• Simple and direct solutions often take more thought and effort to figure out than complicated solutions. But one of the owner's most important jobs is to look for and find simple, direct solutions.

7

ROY'S RULE NO. 6:

Go for Bona Fide Receivables

BUILDING A STRONG CUSTOMER BASE

Without solid, bona fide receivables, you're nothing! They are hard to find, especially in a down economy. But nothing is more important—and nothing will sink you faster than weak receivables. Select only great customers that produce bona fide receivables—receivables that are paid when you want them to be paid.

Roy, isn't any receivable a good receivable?

Not at all. When I talk about "bona fide" receivables, I'm really not talking about printed invoices at all. I'm talking about what owners are in business to do—sell great products and services to great customers, and get paid on time. Isn't that what it's all about? Bona fide receivables come from great customers. And when I say "great" customers, it means they like me and my company, they appreciate our products, and—most important—they pay their bills when we have agreed they will be paid—all the time!

There's nothing more important to your business' survival and success than bona fide receivables. Without solid receivables, you're nothing. Today, all business owners need to work on this, but few give it the attention it deserves. It's like the Holy Grail. If you knew someone was going to find it next Thursday, everyone would be out looking. Solid receivables are getting harder to find. Owners have to pay close attention to this. If you let a staff person select your customers, you're in trouble!

There are a lot of companies around these days, large and small, that seem to think losing money occasionally on bad accounts is the natural scheme of things. Not so. If you have a small company, you just can't afford to lose *any* money. *None.* After all, it's your money. You need to figure out how to serve only great customers who produce only bona fide receivables. Nothing less will do!

What's your basic objective in selecting customers?

I'm from the Midwest where I was always taught the virtues of holding onto one's money—of saving a little bit for the future. I was lucky enough to make good money in my early days as a manufacturers' representative. When I started Southwest Apparel, I used my personal savings to finance the start-up of the business, and I took a fresh approach to my new business. I decided from day one that I was not going to lose any money. Now, there are lots of ways to lose money in a business, but one thing was certain. I wasn't going to lose any money from bad debts. That was just not going to happen. That's how business owners today have to look at their accounts receivable.

To keep from losing money on bad accounts, I have

to do my homework. I really have to be on top our customers, and watch how we turn all our receivables into on-time collections. It all starts with how we are positioned in our marketplace, and how we decide what types of accounts we want to go after. As an owner, I must be involved in these decisions because I am the one who is out there in the marketplace. I'm very selective in deciding which specific customers to do business with and how to get them to pay at a time that is right for my cash flow needs. And then, if something goes wrong—and there is always that chance—I get involved directly with collecting from slow accounts.

I've been fortunate. All my receivables so far have been bona fide. When the bank wants an accounts receivable aging report, I tell them I don't have one. The bank has a fit, of course, but this is partially true, because I insist on collecting all receivables on time—*always*. Nothing is more crucial to me than collecting our receivables when due. I realize that all businesses can't do that. Some have receivables outstanding for 120 days or more. Wow! That's tough on working capital. I don't know how they do it.

Actually, in truth, I *do* have an aging report, but *I don't let it get aged.* I get everyone to pay on time, because they are great customers. They like my products, and they work with me. We get right on top of it. That's the name of the game; getting the check.

Owners really need to establish partnerships with their customers. You are helping them, so they are under an obligation to help you. If they are great customers, they can change their standard ways of doing business to help your company.

Roy, where does it all start?

It starts with product and market positioning. You

may have the best products in the world, but if you sell them in lousy markets that won't or can't pay their bills on time, you're headed in the wrong direction. Many companies have come up with gangbusters products that are really in demand, only to find out later that the nature of the industry they are selling to is loaded with deadbeat collection problems. So how you position your company in the first place is very important if you are going to produce only bona fide receivables. For example, look at all the people who were trying to sell their hot new products into the commercial construction industry in the early 1990s. I shudder to think about their collection problems.

One of your greatest strengths is that you are a smaller business, selling your products to a much larger total market than you could ever hope to capture completely. This gives you the highly desirable option of being selective. Choose only the best markets and customers to do business with. I pity the giant corporations that are so hung up on market share. You realize what that means? They have to go after *all* prospects, deadbeats or not, in order to reach some sort of crazy market-share goal. It's much better to be a tiny pea floating in a great big ocean. If you are a well-run, smaller company, you can choose your shots much more selectively. If you look hard and long enough, you ought to be able to select attractive market segments that produce only solid, bona fide receivables. Don't be greedy.

How do you sort out the good customers from the bad ones?

First of all, you have to know what you are looking for. The way I look at it, a "great" customer is one that likes you, respects your company, appreciates your products, is well positioned in its industry, and especially wants to work with you to your mutual advantage. There are plenty of potential customers out there who look awfully tempting on the surface, but who just don't measure up. Companies who sell to them often live to regret it. They just aren't with you, all the way.

The only way to find these great customers is for you, the owner, to get out into the marketplace and find them. They are few and far between, so it takes some digging on your part and on the part of your sales organization. You can't leave it to your salesmen alone. When you get involved directly, you should be able to establish good relations at the top that add up to sound working relationships for the future. Only you can do that. Too much is riding on it. That's where great customers and bona fide receivables come from. You have to be heavily involved.

Another way to select great customers is to make sure you are going to be able to work with them when something goes awry. If they say, "Sorry, Roy, I'm going to have to pay you in 30 days instead of the 20 we agreed to," you have to be able to work with them and make sure it is 30 days, and not 45. When you agree to extended terms, you get a leg up on them when it comes to prompt payment. If you have a good working relationship, you can then tell them, "Don't *not* pay me." You have to work at that. That is not something that just happens. To do this, you need to have an open channel with the managements and the payables departments of all your accounts. You need to find out when you are going to be paid from their payables department directly.

I took a bit of a gamble once by taking on a major retailer that normally did not pay before 60 days. Plug that into your cash flow! But I knew they were a solid company, and they would eventually pay me. If someone tells you a company is going to pay in 60 days, however, you had better plug 80 days into your cash flow projections. Not that you don't believe them. That's just being prudent.

When I say you have to be selective, I mean you must be prepared to say "no." Many people ask me if I ever tried to sell my "cheap shorts" to a particular national retailer who has been struggling with massive debt. This company was a definite "no." I never tried to sell anything to them, even though they had large potential. I consciously decided not to go after their business because they were not financially secure. That's one of the benefits of being small. I am selective, and that big potential customer just didn't make the cut.

One of my reps asked me to look at a new account the other day. He said that the potential customer had been around for 30 years. I said, "Yeh. So had W. T. Grant!" Times change. People and corporations do crazy things. Select only great customers, or you'll get hurt.

Roy, how do you check out a new account?

First, I check their Dun & Bradstreet rating. You can see if they pay their bills on time or if they are slow. If they are slow, factor it in, or back away.

The next thing I do is see if I can get credit insurance on the account. It's my money. How much do I want to lose? None! Not many owners use this tactic, but credit insurance is available in many industries, and it's a lot better than selling your receivables to some third party, such as a factor. If you can't get credit insurance for a particular account, find another customer. For the low cost of credit insurance, you can't afford to be without it.

Some of my present customers are not covered by my credit insurance company. If a customer can't be covered, I might still do business with them, but I get paid cash in advance to cover my costs. I might gamble with my profit, or I might go for CBD—Cash Before Delivery. But I try not to do that sort of thing very often.

Don't most customers have fixed payment terms?

Nothing in business is fixed forever. If your customers like you and you get along well with them, your customers will help you. Don't be afraid to ask for help. It's easier for me to collect a receivable a few days early from a customer than it is to go to my bank and try to explain why I'm going to be overextended, and beg for more working capital. The nonsense that I'll have to go through with the bank requires far greater effort on my part than the persuasion I can apply to the accounts payable departments of my great accounts. Being a small manufacturer and a valued supplier of theirs usually gets me the relief I need. If the payment terms aren't right for you, and you have a good relationship with your customer, ask for help.

I have had situations in which I have taken business and negotiated the contractual terms of payment. I have even succeeded in changing their payment terms when I could see it was going to be difficult to live with our earlier agreement. Most people think this can't be done. It can be done if you've previously established good relations at the top. You do this by sitting down with your customer's people and explaining the situation, and telling them why you need better payment terms. It's important that you be straightforward. If they can do it, they will try to work with you.

When you really get to know your accounts, you may be surprised to find out that they have many different sets of payment terms for various parts of their business. They might have ten different types, especially if they are of any size, or if they are global. Even smaller customers may have several. You should make yourself aware of all their terms of payment, and go for the best. If you're not satisfied with the terms being offered, only the owner can push for better terms, and actually get something done about it.

Don't forget that you are in a strong position partly because you *are* a small company. You can use the "small fish in a big pond" factor to your advantage. There's nothing wrong with being up-front with your customer. If a surge of business is stretching your cash, for instance, you can certainly say to one of your customers, "My business is really good and my receivables are growing, so I'd really appreciate it if you would pay me a few days early. Thanks for your help!" That's when great customers really show their stuff.

Roy, what happens when even a great customer misses a payment?

We track payments like a hawk. Every day. When a customer's payment is late—even a day—my administrator makes a call. If any problems surface that she can't handle, I'm immediately on the phone to push the collection along. The owner can't avoid doing this. It shows everyone, customers included, just how serious you are about getting paid on time.

Owners want to have their sales forces out in the marketplace, doing their best at closing new business. Many people think, however, that it is somehow inappropriate for sales people to help collect from their accounts. I don't agree. I pay sales commissions to my reps when their products are shipped. But I expect them to act like business people—not just salesmen—and help me collect when there's a problem. In the old days, the financial departments of customers were mysterious things to outsiders. It was common practice to treat the people in accounting with deference. But, they're just like everybody else. If you treat them well and on a business-like basis, you can work with them just like the people in any other department.

Of course, you can go ahead and collect from "slow-pays" the old-fashioned way, and get some ornery, old SOB to call them up and demand payment, intimidating the hell out of them. Frankly, that never made any sense to me. It's too adversarial. It's definitely not the way I like to work with my customers. I would rather have my rep go into their payables department while he is making a sales call, and get to know the department's employees. Engage in small talk. Become a friend, not an adversary. Then, when you need to push a payment along, the rep can say, "It would really help us if you could pay now." They will usually do it. It works!

Customers, of course, have their reasons for not paying. If they want me to finance their businesses, then I'm going to have to factor in more costs on the next order, or drop the account. If they get into financial trouble and can't pay because of a cash crunch, then I have to get involved and work out the best deal I can to secure eventual payment. *The key, though, is not to deal with a troubled account in the first place!*

The bottom line on receivables?

If one of your customers turns sour, drop that company and find another good one. Always be searching for potential customers that are strong in their marketplaces and that pay their bills on time. That's what you want to do—*sell only to great customers in great markets that turn out only bona fide receivables.* Your job is to find great customers. Keep looking!

Everybody says "the customer is king." *If the customer turns out to be a jerk, find a new king!*

The Quick-Study Guide
for Independent Business Owners

GO FOR BONA FIDE RECEIVABLES

- Small companies can't afford to lose money on bad debts. *None!*
- Bona fide receivables come from great customers.
- "Great" customers like you, respect your company, and appreciate your products—and they are happy to work with you.
- Position your company to sell only into strong markets where great customers abound.
- Owners select great customers. That's your job.
- Small companies have a big advantage . . . they can afford to be selective when choosing markets and customers.
- Your goal must be to keep all accounts receivable current. Get on slow-pay accounts immediately.
- Times change. Customers change. Be prepared to drop customers that no longer produce bona fide receivables.
- Be in the marketplace much of the time—looking for great new customers.
- The customer is king. *If a customer turns out to be a jerk, find a new king.*

8

ROY'S RULE NO. 7:

Think Cash

WORKING TOWARDS CONTINUOUS LIQUIDITY

If cash isn't flowing in the right direction for very long, you're company is history! Keeping sufficient cash in the till under all circumstances is vital to your liquidity, and therefore your business' longevity. That's fundamentally what business is all about—reaching a sound level of business where profitability and liquidity are continuous. Only the owner can act on all of the complex relationships that add up to positive cash flow.

Think "cash?" Isn't it better to think "profits?"

You know, I started my business because I saw an opportunity to make money; real money. Now to me, "money" is cash in *my* bank account. I know the accountants need to figure out what my profits are so I can pay my taxes and keep the bank on my side, but I'm mainly interested in the ability of my company to generate more cash than it needs, so I can shift it into my personal account.

The days of pushing for profits alone are over for most

independent businesses. If owners want to be solidly successful, their orientation has to be on cash, and particularly on future cash flows. Cash flows tell you how your cash account is going to change over time. If the cash you need to achieve what you want out of life isn't there, you're in trouble. Profits are important, of course, but you can't eat, spend or invest profits. Only cash pays the piper, and you, and your estate. If you want your company to be a big cash producer, you'd better spend a lot of time thinking about future cash flows and what they mean to your working capital position.

I operate by a fundamental rule. *Everything I decide to do with my company must ultimately result in positive cash flow.* I just won't allow my company to lose money on anything. Then I know I'm strengthening my working capital position, which is what I need to do if my company is to be liquid all the time. This allows me to rely primarily on internal sources of financing to support future business. The ultimate result is solid liquidity and business longevity, along with greatly increased security for the company and, of course, for me. It's the only way to run a smaller business. You can take that to the bank.

What determines which way your cash is flowing, Roy?

For a steady-state company—if there is such a thing— cash flow is directly related to profitability. The higher the profitability, the higher the cash flow. This is true, however, only when you keep a tight rein on your investments in assets. If current assets, facilities or equipment are changing either up or down, that's going to have a big impact on your liquidity. You just might run out of cash. If you do run out of cash, somebody—maybe your banker or a major supplier—is going to take you out of the game. That hurts!

When you have control over future cash flows, you have a chance to be the most competitive outfit in the marketplace, and outstanding profits can result. Owners should remember, however, that *all* the decisions they make to become highly competitive are directly related to their cash flows. You can't operate effectively in the market today unless you think continually of the impact on cash flow of everything you do. If you don't "think cash" all the time, you're going to make some wrong decisions. You need to carry this philosophy throughout everything you do, because everything you do impacts cash, cash flow and working capital.

How do you stay on top of cash flow?

Business is about a lot of things, but most owners are in it for the cash. If you believe that money is power, then cash is what it's all about. Profits are a reflection of what's going on, but they are not the same as cash. If you're not following me, take an executive finance course, like I did. Then you'll know how to steer your ship better.

I didn't start out with a financial background. But every owner needs to know the basics of business finance to succeed. Everyone has certain skills, things they do particularly well. It's very important for owners to develop their strengths, and then work on their weaknesses. Previously, I was a sales and marketing guy, so I didn't pay much attention to finance. I always felt that finance guys were a lot like doctors—you're meant to stay out of their area. Well, I got into their area. I took some finance courses because I wanted to understand. Now I'm no expert, but I sure know where my cash is flowing.

If you're to reach your goals, surplus cash has to be there at some point. Hopefully, when you realize it's importance, the cash will always be there. Everybody says, "Cash is King." That's right. It's so important to me that I personally handle all cash transactions in the company. I receive all collections and make the deposits. I sign all checks that cover our costs and release the funds that cover payroll. It's that serious to me.

A lot has been written about how to stay on top of cash and cash flow. It's the heart and core of any business. If you are in business to make money, you have to be constantly aware of cash flow and your current cash position, day by day. Your cash flow has to be predictable, so you know in advance of any uncovered cash needs that are coming up. Never get into the position where you don't know where you are on cash. It's not all that complicated, but you've got to be on top of cash.

I found, when I started my business, that I needed some special reports that would really help me stay on top of cash and cash flow, so I made up my own. I decided what information I needed, and those are the reports that my company still uses today. I get cash status reports daily. We have excellent general ledger software, and the financial statement reports they produce help me understand where I am on cash and everything else, once a month. But these reports are no substitute for daily cash reporting and making frequent cash flow projections. I couldn't run my business without good cash reporting and forecasting.

Making cash-flow projections is a lot of work. How do you do yours, Roy?

It's vital for an owner to personally make regular projections of cash flow at least quarterly, with monthly updates. Owners need to know the impact the next few months of business will have on cash. I have to know what my cash needs are going to be, and where those funds are going to come from. This lets me know when I need to take special actions to shore up my cash position. I also prepare special cash flow projections when I'm taking on any major new program, like a new, large order, or buying a major piece of equipment. If a new program doesn't make sense on a cash and cash flow basis, it just doesn't make sense to do it.

My cash projections look at cash receipts and disbursements by week over a several month period. They look ahead as far as I can reasonably project solid shipments from scheduled production. I use this report as a basic management tool for smoothing production and providing for short-term cash needs.

I have yet to have one cash flow projection be one hundred percent accurate for more than a week or two. The slightest shift in shipments or piece goods receipts, and the latest report is instantly out of whack. And there are always production glitches. If my projection indicates I'll need $400,000 of short-term borrowings at peak need to cover my working capital requirements, I'd better plan on getting access to $500,000 or $600,000. That's why it really helps to have a little more cash in the till than you think you'll need to do business. Your peak needs will almost always be higher than you thought they would be when doing your projections.

My cash flow projections give me a sense of the direction in which cash will be flowing, now and in the immediate future. I can see from my projections, for instance, that for each million dollars of new business I take on, I'm going to need several hundred thousand dollars of working capital to support the new business up front. What's the major benefit to me? My cash flow projection tells me, "If I don't have it, I don't do it!" Saves me a lot of grief. It's the best tool I have to make sure that positive cash flow *actually happens.*

I keep this information in my head or in a notebook. Some owners may want to be really up-to-date and keep cash flow information in their lap-top computers. This data has to be where you can get at it all the time, because business decisions that directly impact cash flow and working capital are happening all the time. If this knowledge isn't readily available to you, you'll have real trouble making "cash money."

Roy, why can't your accounting department keep track of cash for you?

Owners really need to create their own cash flow projections. Don't ever start thinking that this can be done by your accounting department. It isn't done there. They can put some of the numbers into the projections for you, but you have to make the projections. When you're personally involved, you can be absolutely on top of cash flow. That's the only way to run a business!

People criticize me for keeping accounting people out of cash flow projections, thinking I'm belittling the capabilities of an accounting department. I'm not belittling my accounting department—I never had one! My administrator handles labor productivity accounting, payroll, accounts receivable, payables and all the inputs into the computerized general ledger. So I've made my administrator and computer into what usually passes for an "accounting department."

Accounting and the controllership functions are very important in any company. I constantly discuss our financial results with my operations manager and my administrator. We are the "accounting team." I have an outside accounting firm do our tax returns. But I'm not going to have an outside accounting firm *as well as* an internal accounting department. I don't have a controller, either. The operations manager and I are both "controllers."

The point is, my management team "thinks management accounting," and they also "think cash flow." The result is that by eliminating the need for a traditional accounting department and a controller, I'm probably saving over $80,000 per year. And I'm really on top of cash flow and our cash position.

Where can you put "cash thinking" to work for you?

Probably the best example is when you're sitting there in your customer's office, being Mr. Big. When you're ready to take that $2 million order, you'd better be creating your cash flows at the same time. Before you accept the order, you need to make sure that working capital is available to fund it, and that the profit you need to generate is going to materialize. You find this out by doing a cash flow projection on the spot. It's really important in a sales situation to have all the cash flow numbers you need, wherever you may be. That will go a long way towards making the deal a big success for you.

When I sit down to negotiate, I already have done my homework. I've made sure that we have adequate working capital. I don't have any equipment payments to make, because the equipment needed for the contract is either already paid for or its cost is covered by the contract. I don't have to factor equipment payments into the contract's cost sheet. I don't have a big General and Administrative expense to drag down profits. I've made sure that the overhead needed to service my fixed assets is as low as possible. Nothing extra. No non-productive assets. This is all spelled out in my cash flow projection. With that knowledge at my fingertips, I can tell if I'm going to make good money on the contract.

Most companies really need to have access to more working capital than is readily available to them. We fill our short-term cash needs from our bank line of credit. It's collateralized by our receivables. Our credit line deal is the best, I think, that anyone can get in my industry,

because Southwest Apparel's profits and cash flow performance have been excellent. It's up to the owner to
have adequate working capital available to handle the
order. One way or another, you've got to work this out.
Don't leave it to your accounting department. You do it!

When negotiating a contract, the most important thing
for me is that I don't have any extra costs to be covered
or any cash loan payments to be made. This allows me
to be very flexible in getting the business. I can give a little
on price and still make a good profit on the job. I feel a
lot more secure in determining what I have to do to get the
business. My objective is to get my products from the
machine to the customer as economically as possible. I
don't worry too much about the competition. With my
kind of a cost structure, I *am* the competition.

I was talking to one of my manufacturers' reps this
morning about a new order. He was giving me the items
and numbers while I was translating everything immediately into cash. What the cash needs were going to be,
and what the cash profit would look like at the end of the
project. We just didn't put it into the price-quotation
hopper, like most companies do. I worked it out myself,
and found that we could make an excellent profit on the
contract without any new short-term borrowings. We
took the order.

When you end up with surplus cash, Roy, what do you do with it?

As I said before, I'm in business in the first place
primarily because I saw an opportunity to build a business that could produce more cash than it needed.
Hopefully, that extra cash will go to me, my family and my
estate. But I have avoided falling into the trap of thinking
that, since I own and control the company, my investment
is just as safe inside the business as it would be elsewhere.

That is taking much too much for granted. The world changes. Markets change. Disasters can strike anyone, any time.

It's your business. It's your money. You must decide for yourself how to take advantage of any surplus funds that are created by the business. Solid wealth comes from making investments in productive assets, but there's no rule that says all of those assets have to be in your business. Diversification of risks and common sense argue strongly for investing the major portion of your surplus cash outside of your base business.

Be careful, however. In your eagerness to build productive assets outside of the business, don't rob your company of the balance sheet strength it needs to weather rough times. All businesses face rough times sooner or later. They usually sneak up on you. If you don't keep an adequate level of liquid assets in the business to cover any contingency, you risk destroying your base—your wealth-creating machine. When an adequate safety cushion is in place, then you can take out surplus cash and build an estate that can last beyond your company.

What's the basic point to remember about cash, Roy?

Southwest Apparel is a small but very solid business. We're operating way above our breakeven sales volume. I've been able to take myself off the treadmill by always operating on the basis of strong, positive cash flow. I know where I am on cash, and where I'm going. I can be "choosey." I can go out and get solid, profitable business that isn't "do-or-die" business.

The point is that many American business owners today don't have enough staying power because they're short on working capital, they make tremendous payments for facilities and equipment, they have much too much overhead, and they're not really sure where they stand on cash. By "thinking cash," you have a much better chance of avoiding these problems, and becoming a solid company with staying power—true longevity.

The Quick-Study Guide for Independent Business Owners

THINK CASH

- To be solidly successful, owners must focus as much on cash and cash flow as on profits.
- Learn the basics of business finance. Without that knowledge, solid success will be very hard to come by.
- Every business decision is actually a cash, cash flow and working capital decision.
- Positive cash flow happens only when you keep a tight rein on all assets, both current and fixed.
- Decide up-front that *every* project you take on will contribute to positive cash flow. Allow no loss leaders!
- To be on top of cash, you need to know where you are and where you are going—with respect to cash—all the time.
- Make cash flow projections yourself. Know what your future sources and uses of cash are going to be, and carry that information with you at all times. Don't have your accounting department do this for you.
- It's the owner's job to make sure that adequate working capital is available to support future operations.
- Adjust your cash flow projections every time you take a major order or make any other major business decision.
- For a safer personal estate, invest surplus cash outside the business, but only if the safety of your company's balance sheet is maintained.
- To enjoy solid staying power, "think cash" all the time.

9

ROY'S RULE NO. 8:

Don't Lock In Assets

PUTTING ASSETS TO PRODUCTIVE USES

It would be great to operate a profitable business without the need to fund any assets at all. Nice, but not practical! Most businesses need to employ assets to operate. But owners must make sure that all assets are directly employed in *making money.* Assets that are locked into non-productive uses, such as fancy offices, slow-turning receivables or dead inventories, might just as well be sitting on the moon.

Roy, how do assets get to be locked in?

I've heard it said that the "perfect" company would make high profits with zero investment in fixed and variable assets. That company would have a great return on the assets that are employed by the business, wouldn't it? The only example I know of that comes close to this ideal is the business of renting the use of washers and dryers to apartment dwellers. In the beginning, of course, the owner must invest in the appliances. Some aggressive operators charge enough per load to pay for the equipment in less than six months. After that, the appliances are still on the books, but no money is owed on them. They're depreciable assets, but no payments are required. All in and nothing out, from a cash point of view. If the operation is handled out of the owner's basement with low overhead, it's going to make a ton of money on free-and-clear assets. That's about as close to cash flow utopia as you're going to find.

Most businesses, however, must acquire assets to operate, particularly working capital. The grim truth is that once the owner invests in a range of assets, part or all of them invariably become "locked in." Owned buildings are a good example. When assets are locked in, it's difficult or impossible to use the cash tied up in them for more productive purposes. Like making money.

Many companies have little or no staying power when times turn tough because not enough working capital is available to the business, and because the company isn't generating enough cash flow internally to supply all of its working capital needs. Turning working capital over is how most companies make money. The more your receivables and inventories turns, the more money your company makes. Companies with lots of locked-in assets that can't be converted easily to working capital, such as ancient receivables, dead inventories, or owned equipment they no longer need, can suddenly find themselves in big trouble. Locked-in assets can easily lead to a cash crunch. Not a pleasant thing to happen to anyone!

I believe it can be disastrous for most small business owners to have any significant amount of assets tied up in anything other than good, solid working capital, like bona fide receivables that are going to be collected on time, inventories that are for-sure going to be sold, and good old cash. If any of your assets can't be turned into cash quickly, they are locked in. The accountants consider receivables and inventories "current" if they can be turned into cash in a year or less. The way I look at it, any current asset that takes over six months to turn into cash is locked in and not available to me for making money.

Fixed assets, by their very nature, are more or less locked in. No fixed assets are ever completely locked in, however, because you can always sell land, buildings, or equipment, and turn them into cash—*given enough time.* Time, however, is always the problem. When a company has a powerful need for cash, it's rarely a good time to sell off owned assets. You'll usually take a beating. For all practical purposes, I consider fixed assets to be locked in, so I think a lot about how to be successful with fewer fixed assets at play, and with more working capital making money for me.

Owners must carefully watch how they apply all their assets, keeping as many of them as possible in a liquid form, quickly convertible to cash. As soon as owners start locking in assets, they are reducing their ability to make money, and they may even be starting down the slippery slope to a cash crunch. Most companies don't survive that slide.

What's the big attraction of liquid assets, Roy?

If there is one thing I believe in with a passion, it is having *only liquid assets* in my business. All of Southwest Apparel's assets are liquid. I wouldn't have it any other way. As I said, my accounts receivable are only bona fide, meaning they are one hundred percent collectible when due. None of my inventories are speculative. I admit that I have a leg up on most manufacturers in that I only purchase the materials and supplies needed to make garments that are covered by bona fide orders from my great customers. I also own no buildings. I prefer to lease them. And even though I own all of my production equipment, it's paid for. No equipment payments detract from my cash flow. As it turns out, there's a pretty good market for used industrial sewing machines, so even my production equipment can be turned into cash fast, if it's necessary to sell it.

To be perfectly blunt about it, the ultimate aim of most business owners is continuous and predictable liquidity for their businesses—while generating a few profits along the way. That's where I am today, and that's where I believe any business owner should be. I have real liquidity, because I tie up very little cash in locked-in assets. I keep most of my assets in liquid form, and I put my money into working capital.

You surely need to buy production equipment. Isn't that going to lock in assets, Roy?

To repeat—you only make money from the application of direct labor, so you'd better give your operators the tools they need to make money for you. Having good, efficient, production equipment is essential to getting the highest possible productivity from your operators. But the question always comes up—is it better to lease production equipment or buy it outright? Sure, I could have leased much of my equipment. In some cases, that would have been a good idea, especially when that lets more of my cash work for me as working capital. But I prefer, when I can, to own my production equipment. And I make sure that any new equipment I buy can be paid for out of the operating cash flow of the contract for which it was purchased, after making good money for me and the company.

When owners have available cash, it makes a lot of sense for them to own their production equipment free and clear. The next time you bid on a job that will use that equipment and you do your cash flow projections to see how well you are going to make out, you won't have any equipment payments to figure into your projections. That really helps make you competitive, and gives you a cash safety-cushion that most competitors only dream about.

What about buying non-production equipment?

Again, the philosophy is the same. If the operating cash flow of all contracts in process is really healthy, I try to buy necessary non-production equipment for cash. If it's a very costly piece of equipment, I might consider leasing it, but I would rather die before taking out a long-term loan in the uncertain hope that the equipment will be useful to me for many years. Life is risk. Things can change. Being locked in to a long-term loan for non-production equipment is a risk that I'm just not willing to take. Simple as that!

How do you avoid locking in current assets?

I spend a lot of my time making sure my company doesn't end up with *any* locked-in receivables and inventories. It all starts with selecting only solid, reliable customers that have a strong position in their industries. I make sure I can work with these great customers, which simply means to me that they will pay me on time. Many will even pay me when I *need* to be paid, which may be sooner than their standard terms of payment. I have to be very close to my customers in order to earn this special relationship, so I work hard at gaining their confidence. Otherwise, I'm just gambling with my own money. If I'm ever forced to gamble to get business, then it's time to fold up my tent!

Nothing is perfect, however, and neither are some of

my great customers. To eliminate any risk, I usually sell
only to customers that can be covered with credit insurance. Just to be safe!

I don't have any dead inventory on my books. That
means that we do a terrific job of buying only the materials
needed to fill firm contracts. We buy in just the right
amounts, delivered at just the right times. We may have
to lean on our vendors from time to time, but we get the
job done, because I just can't stand the sight of surplus
inventory. In our business, surplus inventory is locked-
in inventory. I might be able to get some cash out of it,
but I'll lose my shirt on the deal. I don't like any deals that
are not profitable. My administrator understands what
needs to happen. She doesn't let surplus inventory
happen, *ever!*

So, how do you view fixed assets of the buildings-and-land type, Roy?

As I said before, there's absolutely no reason to
acquire any company facilities that are more costly than
the minimum necessary to get the job done. Facilities that
improve the glamour of the company or its prestige
contribute absolutely nothing to running a productive
and profitable business. In most cases, they are counter-
productive.

Of course, I do need to put a roof over the heads of my
operators at the factory. But I firmly believe it is much
better, in most cases, to lease plant and office facilities.
When these fixed assets are purchased, they often tie up
substantial amounts of up-front cash that could go into
making money, or that could safely exit the company into
my bank account for personal investments.

More important, however, owned buildings greatly
reduce my company's flexibility to respond to changes in
general business conditions and opportunities that may

open up in the future. Companies that own their buildings not only have big mortgage payments to make,
they're at the mercy of the commercial real estate market.
I can get out of any of my building leases in less than two
years if I need to move to a location where we can be
more profitable. I like the flexibility that arrangement
provides.

The crux of the matter is that I really don't understand
why anyone would want to own a building, unless you're
in the real estate business, or you have excess money you
don't know what to do with. Maybe you just like to
gamble on commercial real estate. That's not a very good
bet these days. Owned buildings are a big risk. That's
especially true if it's a special-purpose building, or if you
are just starting out, or if you are trying to be lean and
mean. Owned buildings can easily become albatrosses,
and albatrosses can hurt you—big time!

It's like the dilemma faced by a friend of mine. We
were talking the other day about the company building
he owns which was bought to fund his retirement. In the
old days, owners built assets for their retirement by
buying plant and equipment and leasing them back to the
company. They might end up with a $5 million facility,
and it looked good on their balance sheets. But it didn't
really do anything for the business. Buildings don't *make*
money—they *cost* money.

Now my friend's company is struggling, it's having a
tough time making the building's mortgage payments,
and the commercial real estate market has gone to hell in
his area. He's wondering what happened to his great
idea, and to the retirement income that seemed so certain.

Let's face it. I would rather have the cash. I would
rather forego those $80,000 per year mortgage payments
for an overly fancy building, and put extra cash into my
retirement account. It's liquid there —it's cash. You can
always loan it back to the company if you must at some
future date.

Lots of companies have antiquated plants on their balance sheets, and they can't get them off.   The write-downs would kill their statements if they tried. I just don't believe in investing in any nonessentials that don't directly contribute to making money. I need all the cash I can get my hands on to turn into the working capital needed by Southwest Apparel's business. I sure don't want to lock any of that cash into nonproductive uses. When suitable facilities are available to be leased at low rates, I lease them. That's what I'm doing in Tennessee, where I don't have to pay exorbitant wages, and I can get great deals on leased factory space

Some people seem to think that by owning a building, a company is somehow more secure. You can't equate the amount of fixed assets a company owns to its security. Today, a good argument could be made that it's the other way around. Fixed assets can endanger company security. *Too many fixed assets can eliminate company security.* The "perfect" business, as I said, would have none.

I'm not in the real estate business, I'm in the apparel manufacturing business. There's plenty of existing real estate for lease in America today that's suitable for most companies. When I can no longer lease a satisfactory building at a good rate, only *then* would I consider owning a building.

You work hard, Roy, at avoiding locked-in assets. Right?

My goal is to employ mainly liquid assets, especially good solid working capital, in my business. I try to avoid owning facilities wherever I can, and I'm especially not interested in locked-in assets of any type. I don't understand why any company would want to tie up assets for a long time and keep those assets from being used to make money, especially if it doesn't have to.

I don't mean to be trite, but *cash is king!* If you're in business to make money, *you're in business to make money*. You're *not* in business to erect palaces!

The Quick-Study Guide
for Independent Business Owners

DON'T LOCK IN ASSETS

• Locked-in assets can't be turned into cash quickly or easily, so try hard to avoid them.

• Companies only make money by turning over working capital.

• Most companies are short of working capital. Locked-in assets rob a business of the funds needed to make money.

• Fixed assets can usually be considered locked in, for all practical purposes.

• The ideal company has only liquid assets, especially bona fide receivables and saleable inventories.

• The ultimate aim of most businesses is to achieve positive cash flow that is steady and predictable, and that results in continuous liquidity.

• When possible, purchase production equipment with cash that is provided by operating cash flow.

• There's no excuse for acquiring facilities that are more costly than the minimum required to get the job done.

• Don't buy or build facilities if you can lease suitable facilities at favorable rates. Maintain flexibility to deal with change.

• Too many locked-in assets can endanger or eliminate a company's security.

• Put your money into working capital which enables you to make money, and not into owned facilities which cost you money. You're not in business to erect palaces.

10

ROY'S RULE NO. 9:

Avoid Debt Like the Plague

BUILDING FINANCIAL STRENGTH

Create a discipline that leads to profits with longevity by financing longer-term capital requirements from internally generated funds. Relying on long-term debt or outside equity financing can quickly turn into a nightmare, raising costs and very possibly taking away your control over the future of your business.

How does an entrepreneur get started in business without taking on debt, Roy?

Let me be blunt. A fledgling entrepreneur shouldn't go into business without his or her own money in the deal. Many people try it, and they soon find that they've given away their souls scrambling to get start-up financing from outside sources. Part of your original plan has to be to accumulate some seed money before striking out. Don't start a company without being able to put a good shot of your own cash in the project, even if you have to wait a long time before the funds are available. That's what I did. I must have poured in at least $500,000 before my business reached positive cash flow. In my case, cash flow turned positive really fast, but it was my own money that got the business started. No one else's.

The money I put into Southwest Apparel was used to finance my start-up working capital needs and to buy the equipment needed to get started. To try to get that kind of money externally, short of family and friends, is very, very difficult, although not impossible.

The benefit of starting your business this way is that when you have no debt at start-up, you can begin immediately generating operating cash flow, and then you can continue building the business with that flow of cash. When it's your own money in the deal, you are totally focused on making the business profitable from day one. That's the only way to operate during start-up.

In some start-up situations, however—like starting a wholesale distributorship, for example—you may need to get a bank line of credit for inventories and other working capital needs right from the start. That kind of money is both hard to get and very expensive. Plus, you had better have deep pockets, because the bank will try to collateralize that loan with everything in sight. The bottom line? Try hard to finance your initial working capital requirements yourself.

Basically, most start-up companies aren't bankable. If the bank won't step forward and you can't fund it yourself, you're left with equity funding—private placement funds or venture capital—as alternative sources of money. Equity financing might work for the brilliant engineer who is developing the greatest whiz-bang widget in the world in his laboratory where the funds required for start-up are huge—in the millions. If you're on to something big, venture capitalists will be all over you. Of course, I would never dream of raising capital that way, because success to me means being in personal control of my destiny and my business. If you want to be in control of your life, resorting to a private placement or venture capital sources is the surest way to lose control!

How do you view using internally generated funds versus finding external sources?

Someone told me a while back that there are only four sources of funds available to finance a business. They are cash flow from internal operations, reductions in assets—like selling off surplus equipment or reducing receivables, increases in debt, and increases in equity investments. The first two, I like. The last two can mean trouble.

I decided from the beginning that I would try to finance everything I needed to get my company off the ground from my personal assets, and then, once the company was launched, to use internally generated funds to build the company to where I wanted it to be. That's a basic philosophy of mine. Think about it. The more you avoid using *any* form of external financing, the better off you're going to be. If you succeed, your debt carrying charges are going to be low, and you're going to be in total control—no questions asked.

The availability of external financing is another problem. It has a bad habit of coming and going, and the future cost of that money is out of an owner's control. If possible, I feel you're much better off relying on your company's internal financing resources. You just cannot and must not put yourself into a position where you *must* rely on the "money brokers." They can eat you alive! Being at the mercy of the money brokers can mean losing your self-respect, your ability to control events, and your ability to make the company work for you. And after all, isn't that why most business owners take the risk of operating a company in the first place? So the company will work for them?

I use mostly internally provided funds to finance current operations, acquire equipment and other fixed costs, and particularly to finance what little growth I allow. Growth has the bad habit of consuming large amounts of working capital. Of course, to make it possible to use internal funding exclusively, I've made sure that my current operations are producing solid results at the gross profit level, and I've forced my overhead expenses down to industry-low levels. This is where solid success begins for me.

Be very, very careful when you do use external funding of any type. All forms of external financing, particularly debt, can quickly become your enemy. They raise costs, possibly take away your control over the future of the business, and they may even keep you from achieving your personal goals. Successful owners I know use external financing very reluctantly, and, if they must use it, *very carefully.*

Everybody needs a good credit line from their bank though, don't they, Roy?

I try like crazy to avoid using *any* debt financing—either short-term or long-term debt. It's been said that, "He who controls your working capital controls your business." The only exception I make is for short-term working capital financing. A working capital line is a healthy use of debt, although it may only be available to you once your business has reached positive cash flow. Even then, you should use that form of debt only when you're absolutely certain that the loan can be repaid in weeks, or at the most in a few months. Banks have an interesting habit. They like to get paid off.

But even when your company is operating on solid

ground, it's wise to keep a revolving bank credit line open for your potential use, since you never know when an opportunity may arise that could not be pursued without it. If you are highly profitable and largely self-financed, you'll be surprised how low an interest rate can be provided by your friendly banker.

It seems today that debt has become a permanent part of most businesses. Short-term and long-term debt. In the old days, owners used their own funds to finance working capital and other short-term needs. Lately, many companies have been financing working capital with short-term debt. They do this to earn a better return on the equity they have in the business, and it works fine as long as they are able to pay the working capital loan back when due. Some owners find, however, that they can't pay off their credit lines when they had agreed to with the bank. In effect, they are treating short-term debt as if it were long-term debt. When that happens, your banker just might suggest that you convert your "evergreen" working capital loans into term debt. That can be a real shocker. Those principal and interest payments can kill a business.

With new bank regulations, owners must now clean up their working capital lines for 30 days every year. Suddenly, the owner realizes that the dead inventory out there in the warehouse isn't going to go away—the bogus inventory that can't be cleaned up. Now, all of a sudden, the owner *must* clean it up. "Oh, Oh! Here's trouble!"

How much, then, should an owner rely on internally generated funds?

I'd say, "completely." Sooner or later, every business is going to run into a glitch. *Absolutely every business is going to have a glitch!* I don't give a damn if it's once every year, or once every twenty years. The time will come when you need some solid help financially, and you're going to have to rely on your own resources. Imagine, *your own resources!* That's when having no debt, except for justifiable working capital debt, is the *only* position to be in. By relying too much on external financing, you can very easily become overwhelmed, you'll lose control, and your capital sources will start running your business.

A terrific thing happens when you force yourself to avoid debt like the plague. Living by this philosophy means that you must finance everything you want to do with your company entirely from the cash generated by internal operations, plus a limited credit line. When you do this, you've created a built-in restraint that can lead to high profitability and, most important, business longevity. It's as if it is "nature's way." This check on your decision-making produces a really successful business equation for making money. It keeps you from getting yourself into trouble. It tells you, "Hey! It's your business and your money. You've reached your limit. Stop!"

I take it, Roy, that you're not a fan of long-term debt. Right?

I have no long-term debt, and I intend to keep it that way. I don't want to be like the owner who owns his company's plant and equipment, and hopes that, when he retires in twenty years, he will get $2 million for it after all the long-term debt has been paid for. This guy has a much prettier plant than I do. In a much nicer section of town than mine. So that's what he's going to end up with. A nice 40,000 sq. ft. plant somewhere. But that plant is probably only worth something as an ongoing business, and it may not be ongoing when he's ready to liquidate.

I'd rather be the guy who ends up in twenty years with $2 million in his retirement fund and no long-term debt— and with a solidly successful, cash-producing business.

That's worth something!

Debt was the way of the 1980s. Money was too available—too tempting. It was possible to build a \$1 million plant and borrow \$999,000 on it. Sometimes, you could get \$1.2 million for it. It all depends on what you want to do. Do you want to build bricks and mortar, or do you want to build liquid assets?

When is it a good idea to use lease financing?

Leasing equipment locks you into payments that hit your cash flow, and that can be bad. There may be times, however, when the equipment you need to make your direct labor productive cannot be financed internally. Then, lease financing might make sense if the cost isn't too high.

One of the things that has gotten a lot of companies in trouble today is carrying everything to the "nth" degree— getting carried away with every new idea and trend. If someone makes a good argument for leasing a building or equipment, right away the owner wants to lease everything—lease the cars, lease employees, lease a customer, lease a spouse . . . lease *everything*. Next thing, your balance sheet shows 90% lease debt. Or, what's better than 90%? How about 100%? It just doesn't follow!

If I have to acquire a piece of production equipment to make money, however, and if I don't have the cash at the time, then I may just have to lease it. I'd prefer to buy it, of course, from operating cash flow. Then I wouldn't have payments to make on the stuff, and I'd be a lot better off than the guy who has to make payments. Plus, that equipment can be a nice little nest egg. If I ever get into trouble, I can always get financing on it to help out in a cash crunch. In a sense, it's like a liquid asset, because it is not security for anything—a note or a lease. It's mine.

No payments!

But when you decide to use lease financing for equipment, you must realize that when you lease that equipment at 14%, and you come up against a competitor that doesn't have to make those big lease payments, then something is going to have to give. You're going to have to take less profit or be more efficient somewhere else. You're just not going to be as competitive as the other guy unless you own the equipment—and it's paid for.

Some small business owners have an urge to go public. How about equity financing?

I believe that all successful businesses need to have certain basic strengths. One of these is to have a good banking relationship. I don't care if it's with Harris Trust, or Merrill Lynch, or First Industrial Bank. You need this for yourself as the owner, and also for your business. When you go out to kindle that relationship, you have much more strength if you are a solid, stable little company, producing a lot of cash, with you in total control of the business. With that going for you, you probably won't ever need outside equity financing.

But what if someone were to offer to put $1 million into my company for a 49% ownership interest? That might appear to be a tempting proposition, because it would make my company seem even more solid financially than it already is. But for me, that deal is just like selling out, and it puts a partner into the saddle with me. Partnerships just don't work. The worst partnership to have is one with a family member or your best friend. That kinship or friendship can disappear in the heat of battle. If you think you need outside equity partners, go public. Let your "partners" be faceless.

Most companies can't get equity financing from anyone when they are small and have few growth prospects, whether they are struggling or prosperous. It's usually when they are on a steep growth curve that anyone might get interested in buying a piece of the action, right or wrong. Most owners who acquire equity financing live to regret it, and most owners who sell out prematurely wish they hadn't. If an outsider owns a piece of your company, you will almost certainly be somewhat subservient to that person. It contradicts what I've been saying about running a solidly successful company. The owner has to be out there in the marketplace, and at the helm—in *total* control. If you have an equity partner, you can forget all that!

I decided a long time ago that since it's my money in the business, I'm going to run the company my way. If you, as an owner, want to do it your way, it has to be your money. If you let somebody in with their money, and money talks, you relinquish control. You're answerable to the money source!

So, you would just prefer to be self-financed?

It's similar to what I've been saying about having too much staff. Having too many "bosses" fuzzes up control and direction. In a smaller company, one person has to have the vision and run the company personally.

I'm not in love with banks, but really a banker is a better "partner" for an owner than an equity investor. Bankers have been very helpful to me, but they don't control my company as long as I meet their terms. I'll do anything to avoid having an equity investor sitting in the office next to me, looking over my shoulder. When I'm in total control, it's much easier for everyone to figure out who makes all the most important decisions. It's me, and it's only me. There's less chance for confusion, and a lot less chance for trouble.

What I'm saying is that if you run your company right and finance your company primarily from operating cash flow, you won't need long-term debt, and you certainly won't need an equity investor. Your business will be your bank. You'll be able to build a successful business and lead a wonderful life. *And you can keep it all yourself!*

The Quick-Study Guide
for Independent Business Owners

AVOID DEBT LIKE THE PLAGUE

• Start your business with your own money. If you haven't accumulated enough, wait and save for another day.

• It's far better to obtain operating funds from the cash flow generated by internal operations or possibly by reducing assets, rather than increasing debt or equity.

• Work towards 100% internal financing of all funding needs, except for short-term, working capital needs.

• Keep a revolving bank line open for your potential use in seizing opportunities.

• Restricting yourself to using only internal financing sources for acquiring assets becomes a built-in guide to profits with longevity.

• External financing sources—debt and equity—are notoriously unreliable as to availability and cost.

• Don't put yourself in a position where you must rely on the "money brokers." He who controls your working capital controls your business.

• Pay off your revolving bank credit line as soon as possible, but always within a year.

• You're in business to build liquid assets, not bricks-and-mortar. Avoid funding anything with long-term debt.

• Leasing productive assets can be useful, but realize that you are at a major disadvantage compared to the competitor who doesn't need to make lease payments.

• Equity partners are like most partnerships. They don't work, and you can lose control.

11

ROY'S RULE NO. 10:

Keep Pushing Productivity & Quality

MAXIMIZING EFFICIENCY AND VALUE
Productivity and quality are never fixed quantities. They can always be improved, and they must be for your company to remain competitive. If you want to be a solidly successful force in your marketplace, you must search for operating practices and equipment that will increase the efficiency of your personnel and improve the quality and resulting value of your products and services. Keep pushing hard for continual improvements in productivity and quality.

Everybody is pushing productivity and quality. Why are they such critical issues to you, Roy?

Productivity and quality are completely intertwined with profitability. An owner has to build a business that is very good at both in order to be competitive and make good money. Let's face it, productivity and quality are two vital aspects of running a very efficient company that makes great products for its great customers—one that ends up with lots of extra cash at the end of the month. They are both prerequisites to profits and cash flow, and an owner has to keep pushing all the time to improve them. Productivity and quality just have to be there, or profits surely won't be. While trying to be very good at both, I keep all my costs down to the bare-bones minimum. That works for me.

When I'm deciding how to make my business as successful as possible, I think a lot about *total productivity*. The way I look at it, there are three vital elements of *total productivity*; equipment, people, and quality. To be totally productive, I work on having the most productive and efficient equipment, processes and practices in my production and administrative areas. Next, I think about the productivity of all my people; workers, staff and managers, and especially myself. Then I consider the quality of the products we produce and the value they provide to our end consumers. If Southwest Apparel isn't producing the highest quality products in my market, all the productivity in the world won't do me any good.

To make my company totally productive, I have to make sure that everyone is measured, and every task is measurable. If I don't measure all the inputs and outputs of my processes, I'll never know how productive we are, or what needs to be tweaked to improve results. It's as simple as that. Everything important has to be measured.

What about buying production equipment to make your manufacturing processes more productive?

Owners have to know what production equipment to buy, and when to buy it. They should work with their people to obtain the *right level* of equipment for optimal production and worker productivity. That level, however, does not necessarily make your direct labor as productive as it possibly could be using unlimited resources. You have to aim for the *right* level of productivity, not the *highest possible* level. Otherwise, you'll end up with equipment overkill, and that can be a lot more harmful than helpful.

In my business, a typical order is a contract for several thousand dozen items of a particular design, to be delivered to a retailer's stores over the several months of a season. Sometimes I'm faced with a situation where I can't take the contract without buying additional sewing machines. It's tempting to assume the customer will continue ordering that product after the first contract, and the new equipment will therefore be in use over a long period of time. If that turned out to be the case, I could take my time to recover the cost of the new equipment. Bad idea. Bad gamble.

The way I look at it, I need to see if the full cost of needed production equipment will be paid for out of the *operating cash flow of the contract*. If so, and there is cash left over, I buy it and take the contract. If it can't be paid for from the contract's cash flow, I don't buy it, even if that means we don't take the contract.

The last thing business owners need is to have a lot of idle equipment on their hands because they figured their equipment needs wrong, or they gambled. When they are forced to keep making lease or term debt payments on excess equipment, their projected cash flow is going to take a hit. Don't become equipment-poor, like most of our farmers in America became a few years ago. They were just working to make the payments on their equipment. If you run the numbers and it turns out that after six years of making payments on your new equipment you finally start making money, forget it! You might as well go on down the road and work for McDonalds. That's no way to run a productive and profitable business. When I look at a million dollar contract and I can't see how that contract will pay for the equipment I need to produce the products, I'm not going to take the order. I'd rather pass.

I realize, of course, that all businesses aren't in the same position that I'm in. Companies with product lines that will be around for a few years usually can't pay for their equipment needs from the net operating cash flow that comes from their first orders. Those companies, however, have to really work at keeping their equipment investment to an absolute minimum so that it is paid for within a year. If your company is subsidized by the government, or is public, or has some outside funds to play with, it can pay off its equipment over a longer period. But if you're operating with only your own funds, a longer payback period is a crazy risk to take in most industries.

If you are considering a production equipment purchase with a long payback period, make sure you are entirely familiar with trends in the marketplace that could eliminate the future need for the equipment before it has paid for itself. Otherwise, your business might become like so many companies today—fixed-asset rich, and cash poor. You'll be looking out in the shop at a row of monuments to foolish gambles.

When I started Southwest Apparel, I bought the equipment I needed to fill our first orders from my own funds. We made a profit on those first orders, and I didn't have to worry about lease or loan payments for that equipment.

Of course, if an owner can avoid buying extra equipment and still fill the order, that's best for your cash and working capital situations. I recently took additional business that would normally require the purchase of more equipment. I did not feel good about adding equipment at the time. But because I have such terrific customers, I was able to get the deliveries rescheduled to stretch them out, and I avoided the need for additional equipment.

Owners need to take a look at all facets of a contract and try to schedule things so any equipment purchases that seem to be required are really justifiable. At some point, you might decide you would rather have $25,000 in the bank or in the kids' college fund, instead of in equipment. If, by rescheduling deliveries, you're able to avoid buying equipment now, that's the way to go.

How do you evaluate non-production equipment that could improve overall productivity?

The productivity of direct labor, of course, comes first, so I get excellent production equipment for my operators, but not necessarily the latest-and-greatest that's available. For other types of supporting equipment, such as computers for improving administrative efficiency, the productivity I'm talking about is getting people to perform better, whether it's producing more output, being on the job with less sick days, or having a better attitude. In order for that to occur, a small company can take advantage of equipment that is both productive and reasonable, whether it's for the payroll department or the foundry.

It's a question of priorities. How important is it for you to have the latest-and-greatest "toys" at your plant? Then you can bring the boys over and say, "Hey, I've got this new set of golf clubs, but I can't drive the ball any further!" Many owners are on that kind of an ego trip. Now that's all right, as long as somewhere down the road, you and your company aren't going to need the fifty grand you invested in that new equipment. My point is, keep the fifty grand. You can always buy equipment. There will always be the latest-and-greatest.

I always try to keep using a piece of equipment that is performing its function for as long as I think it is making a satisfactory contribution to productivity. The key is to continue benefiting from the productivity improvements already being provided by your current equipment for as long as possible. That's the best way to optimize your total productivity cost per employee. Newer technologies keep coming along. Be patient, and be careful.

If I see, however, that I will be able to bring some big bucks to the bottom line by putting in new equipment, that's what I'll do, especially if it means that I can get the job done with fewer people. In America today, if you can eliminate a person, you've got to do it. That's reality. Hopefully, that new equipment will help make your company more productive, add to your company's longevity, and keep your remaining employees employed longer.

When I started Southwest Apparel, the operations manager and I went to the big Bobbin Show in Atlanta to see what type of computer system made sense for us. We contacted a number of computer companies. We even looked at IBM. They gave us the big IBM song-and-dance. Put us in their auditorium. Pretty soon, they were talking about a System 36—over $100,000 worth of hardware, software and support. We could very easily have spent a couple hundred thousand dollars that day.

It would have been nice to have an IBM System 36. It would have performed all the needed functions, but we decided to punt. At the time we had access to a Tandy "$800-special." The operations manager brought it in from his house. We started by programming the Tandy to do our work, but then we upgraded to a PC clone. At the end of the first year, our total investment in a computer system was $14,000, including software. We had plenty of horsepower to do our own payroll, piecework tickets, and many administrative tasks with that simple system. The operations manager did most of the programming. Talk about self-reliant! We've gotten a lot of work out of that simple, inexpensive computer system. *The key to that purchase was "sufficiency."* It did the job for us.

We look at new computers and other support equipment all the time, but you have to remember that the computer's already been invented. The 286 chip in our computer is a little slow, but it does everything we need to get done in a reasonable time frame. The 386 microprocessor is a little faster, and the 486 chip is faster yet. Really, though, the basic functions of these systems remain the same. If an owner can put in a new computer system and eliminate the need for five people, fine. But, if you go out and spend $100,000 on new computers without eliminating any additional people, has that made you any more productive? Has it done anything for the bottom line? Probably not.

My point is that it's easy to end up with tremendous equipment overkill. That happens to a lot of companies with both office and manufacturing equipment. Spending money on productivity-improving equipment and working on improving productivity with what you have or can get cheaply are two very different things. It's a gut management decision. You have to make it.

How do you actually decide whether or not to buy a new piece of equipment?

First of all, I forget the Wharton School thing. I don't do a sophisticated discounted cash flow analysis on every piece of equipment I'm thinking of buying. If a smaller company has the capabilities on board to do that kind of analysis, it's probably over-staffed.

You need to ask yourself three questions about new equipment. First, is the new equipment absolutely necessary for you to execute a contract that you already have? If so, it's a slam dunk. It takes the highest priority. Second, will the equipment substantially improve the productivity of direct labor? You look at this a lot more carefully, because maybe it will and maybe it won't, over the long run. Third, will the purchase just make the company work more smoothly? This has nothing to do with the productivity of direct labor, so you scrutinize it very carefully. Unless it has some overwhelming impact on your business, you're probably not going to do it.

When a project passes this first rough test, then you should do a cash flow projection to see if you can pay for the new equipment from the operating cash flow of the project for which it is required, or certainly in less than a year. If it does, consider it. If it doesn't, forget it. Save your money for something that really counts.

There will always be something out there that is better than what you have right now. The owner has to lead the management team through the buy or not-buy analysis— looking at better and alternative ways of doing things, and deciding what is worth doing now. They need to have a strong voice in the decision. You can't dictate all decisions for them. If you do, your employees will feel powerless and morale will take a big hit.

If, for instance, a manager wants a $10,000 piece of software for our pattern-making operation, I go through the whole process with those involved, step by step. I get them to look at all sides of the issue. When I do that, sometimes they just come right out and say, "Hey, it's not really necessary to get this now." Then the decision to drop it is their decision.

When we looked at that $10,000 piece of software, we asked ourselves, "Will it do more than we can do now?" Of course. "Would you like to have it?" Sure. "Do we really need it?" Well, it really isn't going to improve the quality of our product. It isn't going to save any people. "Is it going to make us any more productive?" Maybe it will help, but not by much. It would have been great to do our pattern-making a little faster. But the bottom-line return on the incremental improvements just wasn't there. So the management team decided not to buy it now. That doesn't mean, of course, that we won't take another look at it later.

I believe it's important that the people who actually work on the equipment play a major role in making a decision to buy new equipment. As the owner, I ask all my people, "Is there anything you need that would help you do a better job?" If they tell me they need something, and we discuss all the angles with the managers and people involved, and it strikes me that, in the final analysis, it would help them a lot, I get it for them. But we had better be sure it can be bought out of operating cash flow, and that it isn't just "nice" to have.

Owners must keep looking for ways to improve productivity, but they have to be very cautious about spending money on new equipment. What you currently use may be sufficient and more than adequate. That new stuff just may not pay.

How else do you improve the productivity of your direct workers, Roy?

Most people, of course, prefer to take home a pay check and not be measured. I understand that. In today's competitive marketplace and very competitive world, piecework systems for direct labor and performance-based incentives for other employees can be designed to reward your high achievers. Many theorists are against piecework. Just as many companies are putting managers on pay-for-performance plans, some are taking similar incentives away from production workers. That doesn't make sense to me.

What does make sense to me is to reward all of a company's super-performers for superior performance, whether they are managers, supervisors or operators. I do this by setting up performance-based total compensation programs for everyone. Of course, I need to provide my employees with a nice work environment, and I make sure they are being listened to by me and by their supervisors.

Companies are always going to have certain employees who are better performers—people who want to get ahead more than others. Some, however, just want to get along and get their paychecks. People are different. They're not homogenized. But in designing incentivized total compensation programs, you have to realize that owners can't afford to pay employees the wages today that were paid in years gone by, and we can't afford to pay non-productive people at all. The global economy has made that very clear. Production and productivity are now measured. It has to be that way for a company to survive.

I represented companies in the old days that are gone now. Bankrupt. They did a good job of serving their customers, but they were not as productive as my company is today, or as productive as manufacturers have to be in this competitive world economy. Everything is engineered by minutes. Labor productivity has to be there. I don't make up the numbers.

The total compensation package I provide for workers must allow my company to compete in the global economy. I can pay no more. No business owner can. The right compensation level can vary somewhat, of course, with the level of your productivity-improving equipment investment and prevailing wage rates. If local labor conditions require direct labor compensation levels higher than the upper limit needed to stay competitive, your plant is in the wrong location. You had better start looking for a new location for production, either in the United States—perhaps in a smaller, rural town—or offshore, if necessary.

Have you tried using worker teams to improve labor productivity?

Some "experts" suggest organizing workers into teams to make them more productive. We have a team, all right. A very small team. Ten people—our few managers, an administrator, and our supervisors. That's our team. It's important for me to have *that* team. It is *not* important for me to have a league of teams. There's a difference. Some consultants want your employees to be in a team, on a team, near a team, about to get into a team. *I'm not interested!* Why? It just doesn't work. If any workers feel an urge to be part of a team, they should join a softball team after work!

Every operator on our production lines moves the product along the line to the next operator. If two people don't get along, that doesn't mean the two of them can't do their separate jobs very well. That doesn't mean they can't respect one another. And they don't have to go bowling together at night if they don't want to. Some consultants are trying to take the team concept to an extreme. They are fuzzing up the chain of command. When "teams" take over, it's not clear who is responsible individually for what. Think about it. People can barely get along with their families, let alone with a company team. The team concept is utopian. Like most utopian ideas, they usually don't work in the real world.

For complex manufacturing and assembly processes, it may be desirable to use a team approach with employees at higher worker compensation levels. This method may result in lower turnover and better productivity. But it won't work for me, in my type of manufacturing business. So be careful about following the crowd and adopting every new management theory. That can really screw up your great operation.

Why do I say that? There's something happening in America today that suggests that it's almost un-American

to measure anyone's performance. People are just supposed to show up? Have a nice working environment?
Make sure that nothing is going to fall on their heads or
hurt them? And then, of course, they're supposed to get
a full basket of benefits?

Well, excuse me! That won't work! That's the
government's world, not the world of manufacturing.
That will not work! That doesn't mean an owner can't
have a group of employees working closely together in a
nice environment—each individually responsible for
getting his own job done right, and incentivized to be as
productive as possible. That does work!

How do you make your management team as productive as possible?

The answer to that question can be found in selecting
highly self-reliant people for management positions, and
giving them the right incentives. Discretionary bonus
programs seem to work well for attracting and holding
productive managers. The amount of annual bonus I pay
each manager is based on the overall profitability of the
company, as well as the individual's performance during
the year. We pay out some pretty handsome discretionary bonuses annually, and their effectiveness shows up in
how well our management team is motivated. They're
fantastic!

As a small company, I decided from the beginning that
I just wasn't going to have any "middle management"
crap. We only employ people who actually do productive things, and not one person whose job it is to just help
others do things.

Look at all the large and small companies that are still
loaded down with too much middle management! In
some companies, middle managers can actually rise to
the top without having done anything meaningful on the

job. Think about it. Think of all those management-types today who are sitting in board rooms without having actually *done* anything of consequence in their lives. And, of course, they have no clue! In too many large companies, being a manager no longer has anything to do with performance, ideas or vision. Small companies can't operate that way and be solidly successful. We surely don't.

That's why I've never added any "middle" people. Besides, I can't pay them enough to have them want to come and work at Southwest Apparel every day for 20 years. They would need to move on to get ahead. I recognize this requirement for what it is. Owners can afford to pay only so much for management and still be competitive in the world economy. That's reality today. By eliminating as much overhead as possible, you can pay your management team quite well. That's how you attract and hold your few, outstanding, productive managers.

How do you manage to compete so effectively in the world economy?

Most of the simpler manufacturing jobs in America have been going offshore. Companies just don't need to pay someone $17 an hour to put bumpers on cars. It's as simple as that! Look at the layoffs happening at General Motors. GM workers in Mexico earn $2 per hour putting on bumpers, and the GM workers in Ypsilanti are getting $17 per hour, with plenty of benefits. That's hard to fight. As a highly successful entrepreneur said recently, "Einstein couldn't run a factory and compete with that!"

The point is there are limits to the amount of wages you can pay for simpler manufacturing tasks and still be competitive in the world economy. You either have to find a cheaper source of relatively low skilled domestic labor, make existing labor more productive, or pack your bags and look for offshore sources of labor. Many companies have not found their manufacturing labor solution offshore yet, but they are searching. If they can't improve labor productivity enough in the United States, many will eventually have to use offshore manufacturing labor to stay competitive.

This trend is sure to eliminate the majority of the lower skilled manufacturing jobs in America. When you take away a worker's ability to make a decent wage, that person can't even purchase the products produced with offshore labor, let alone domestically produced products. This is tough talk, but business owners have to look at it realistically. It's their money.

The only way I know to compete in the world economy, using American labor for simpler manufacturing jobs, is by measuring everything, and by providing an incentive for my operators and all my people to excel by becoming extraordinarily productive. That's why every single direct and indirect employee of Southwest Apparel is on an incentive compensation program.

I strongly believe in this approach to maximizing productivity. It would be a lot easier to pay everyone an hourly wage, and let them proceed at their own pace. That might make sense for some companies. But in today's competitive climate, an incentive pay system is one of the best ways to reward those workers who are willing and able to work hard and efficiently. When that happens, they win and you win, and the company is still in the ball game.

My performance is measured by the company's bottom line, so it makes sense that everyone's performance be measured, one way or the other. They all have to perform—the supervisors, the operations manager, the workers, everyone. They must perform, because the plant must be profitable. I simply won't have it any other way.

As I have said, our managers receive an annual bonus based on performance, productivity and company results. But how do I measure my administrator? The administrator runs the whole payroll "department" herself. The payroll has to be accurate, or the incentive programs won't work. She buys piece goods. We can't end up over or under. If she makes a mistake, it is very apparent. Therefore, everyone's performance—even hers—is measured, and that becomes the basis for incentive compensation payments.

Line supervisors get a daily incentive, based on their line's results that day. They also can make extra money every week, based on a formula that is related to production and productivity. Each supervisor is highly incentivized to replace quitters fast, get them trained and up to production fast, or, if they don't make it, get them out the door fast and find some better workers.

It all boils down to this. To compete in world markets, owners must get maximum productivity from everyone in their companies. You do this by pushing productivity constantly, acquiring plant and equipment investments that will significantly improve the efficiency of your production processes, but that won't put you in the hole financially. Give all your workers good, responsive management, good working conditions, useful equipment and a good incentive compensation program, and your managers and operators will work hard and be extraordinarily productive. That's how I win in the global game. Other companies can win the same way.

Roy, how does product quality fit into all of this?

To me, having the highest quality products is a given. Everybody is looking for value, and value usually equates to quality and price. Quality simply must be built into your products. If it isn't, your business will not survive, or at least you won't be as solidly successful as you should be. I can't imagine anyone succeeding with low quality, even if you have high productivity. It won't work. Productivity and quality must go together.

Though we have excellent quality now, I always want our quality to get better, so I work on improving quality constantly. I could care less about meeting the so-called "standards of the industry." I don't know or care about the standards other manufacturers are trying to meet. Whatever they are, we must do better.

The way I look at it, our quality has to be the best, independent of what I charge for our cheap shorts. It does not follow that if our shorts sell for less, they need to be less well made. Our shorts are economically-produced, high-quality shorts. We use only the best threads, elastic and piece goods. We use excellent sewing equipment. Sometimes our material costs are higher than our competitors', so we must sew our garments more economically. Similar shorts of the same quality are on the market. Some have to be sold for more money because they can't be produced as economically as ours.

It kills me, though, to have any of our shorts sewn improperly, especially when I have gone to all the trouble and expense to buy the best fabrics and acquire excellent equipment. We keep working on the operators' proficiencies and the inspectors' techniques. In fact, we work on quality all the time. Most companies just work within tolerances. We constantly measure the quality of what we are making, so we know it's the best quality available before it is shipped. When it comes to product quality, "adequacy" and "sufficiency" just don't fly.

The most important thing to me is how the product looks when it comes out of its carton—when the end customer first sees it. I always want it to look the best. I'm never satisfied. Even though we have a low return rate,

I'm always working on improvements. Hopefully, the customer thinks our products look great. If an end user thinks they don't look so great, I want to know about that, so I can do something about it.

Does our product quality help me get orders? You bet it does. Everyone is aware of how well our products perform in the marketplace, especially the buyers of the big retail chains. That's a measurable standard, and they measure it. It is quite obvious to them if we are producing quality products, or if we aren't. There's no place to hide!

What do you do, Roy, when a quality problem occurs?

Owners can really distinguish themselves from mediocre companies through responsive customer service, especially when a customer discovers a quality problem. When a problem occurs, an owner must do something about it immediately. Go to the source of the problem and rectify it. Even if the quality of most of your products is excellent, don't hesitate. Ship the bad stuff back to the factory and fix it. Address the problem immediately.

It's especially important that you not question the customer's judgement. If the customer perceives it's a quality problem, *it is a quality problem.* Don't screw around by sending it to a laboratory and telling the customer that "we will look into it." That's the kiss of death. That's what all his other suppliers say. Be different. Just get on an airplane. Go to the customer. Fix the problem, fast. It's one of the best opportunities you'll have to be a hero in the eyes of that customer.

I had a quality problem recently. A store laid out my products and they looked awful. I said, "Send them *all* back." They got by the inspectors, the managers—everyone! They were not all bad, but there were some in a few cartons that looked really awful. So we took them all back. We went through every carton, and reinspected every item. We fixed the items that needed fixing. The whole factory knew what was happening—the operations manager, the operators and inspectors, everyone. This incident made a tremendous impact on the whole factory, and it reminded all of us just how critical it is to make our products right in the first place.

Roy, how about building quality into new products?

I check out every new product we make with our key people. I get our managers to use our products for several months and report on what they find—good and bad. I've set up a simple tracking system so our managers can learn how our new products perform in actual use. That's the best product quality feedback any manufacturer can possibly get. Try getting your managers to do the testing. They will then make sure that quality is built into every product produced.

I take it, then, that pushing productivity and quality really pays off for you?

Whenever we have a production glitch, it proves again to me that there is nothing more important than productivity and quality. What goes out the door and into the hands of customers must be good. Most companies spend excessive amounts of money on overhead and management. All companies would be a lot better off reducing overhead and spending more money on improving productivity and quality, and therefore providing better value to the end consumer. Spend money on the actual *product*—not for outside financing or, God forbid, for management consultants. Don't spend money for fancy facilities or for staff people you can do without. All companies simply must spend the money that's needed to improve the quality and performance of their products.

Some American companies have lost sight of that. If American industry can refocus its wasted overhead dollars on the products it produces, especially on product quality and the total productivity of its operations, the nation's economy will do well again. It's not a question of whether we should do it or not. We *must* do it, because that's what the rest of the world is doing!

I feel that Southwest Apparel today is one of the most productive companies in its industry, producing products of the highest quality. I sincerely believe that—with all due humility. Do we have the most expensive and sophisticated production equipment? *Absolutely not.* If we did, we wouldn't be in business! Adequacy is the key to that.

But when it comes to quality and value provided, are we at the top of the heap? *Absolutely yes.* There's no other way, today, to survive and prosper.

The Quick-Study Guide
for Independent Business Owners

KEEP PUSHING PRODUCTIVITY AND QUALITY

- Productivity and quality must be there, or profits just won't happen.
- Productivity and quality must be improved continuously.
- For productivity-enhancing equipment, adequacy is the key. Avoid overkill.
- For product quality, adequacy isn't good enough. Your products' quality and value provided must be equal to or better than the best.
- To compete with offshore labor, measure every task and every person, and incentivize everyone to be as productive as they can be.
- Give your workers responsive management, good working conditions, useful equipment, and a good incentive compensation program, and they will work hard and be extraordinarily productive.
- Provide monetary incentives for everyone.
- Owners can only afford to provide their managers and direct workers with total compensation packages that allow the company to be competitive in the world economy.
- Be cautious about upgrading equipment. If existing equipment is satisfactorily productive, keep using it. Involve the people who will use new equipment in the decision to buy, or not to buy.
- When a customer discovers a quality problem, the owner needs to jump in personally and fix it, fast.
- Cut overhead costs to the bare-bones. Put those wasted dollars into your products—especially into improved productivity, quality and value provided.

12

ROY'S RULE NO. 11:

Be Very Wary of Growth

TRANSFORMING PERSONAL GOALS INTO SOLID REALITY

Growth is a double-edged sword. It can get you where you want to be with your company, but it can also be a company-killer when "orderly" growth turns into a complete rout. It is absolutely not true that a company must grow, lest it die. Don't bite off more than you can chew. All of the owner's personal goals, including having a wonderful life, can be realized through solid, stable, right-sized operations where profits and cash flow can be maximized.

Roy, what were your goals when you started Southwest Apparel?

When I was traveling through small Midwestern towns as a salesman at the beginning of my career, I noticed that the two guys in one town who seemed to be doing the best were the doctor with the little clinic on the corner, and the business owner who owned the Dairy Queen, the Ramada Inn, and the laundromat. I called on the owner, and I was impressed that he just seemed to keep all his companies plugging along successfully. One of his operations was at one end of town, one was at the other end of town, and the laundromat was in between. He made his steady $200,000 income, year after year. And the doctor at the clinic, he also made his $200,000 every year. The two of them decided what would go on in the town, because they were clearly the solid citizens who got things done. They were the pillars of the community.

It's a good practice for business owners to ask themselves, "Who do I want to be like?" At one point in my career, I decided I wanted to be like the small town doctor and businessman I had seen when I was younger. To me, they were the perfect examples of responsibility combined with success. They had achieved good incomes, financial security, and the life-style they preferred. They were contributing a lot to family and community. That was really important to me, because life is much more than just paying taxes. For me, life is really about making contributions over time. So as I go through life, I don't necessarily ask myself, "*What* do I want to do?" It's more, "W*ho* do I want to be like?"

I have always admired these two guys, because they were successful over time. They have been achieving *solid success with longevity.* That's the key. That's the real skill. Create something of value, and then plug along at a steady pace, keeping it successful and profitable, year after year. It's the American dream—the small business owner putting something back into the world. Creating jobs. Transforming personal goals into solid reality. That's what makes life exciting for me. This "grow-or-die," "go-for-the-big-bang" attitude so many have, and then go live in Bermuda for the rest of your life—give me a break! It doesn't work!

But if I grow my company, I'll make more money and create more jobs. What's wrong with that, Roy?

People have asked me why I'm content to continue selling $5 million a year of "cheap shorts," and not build Southwest Apparel into a much larger company. I certainly could. The market is there, and my position with my customers could help make it possible, if that were my goal. But I don't want to grow my business! I really don't have a strong urge to become the owner of a $25 or $50 million company. In fact, I really don't think much about gross receipts. It would be a great disservice to my company, my family, and myself to become obsessed with pure volume and growth. I get a real kick out of making a good product, getting an order and getting it shipped. I like to have a product that does well in the marketplace. If I can't do that and make money also, I should go lay down on the railroad tracks—and wait for Big Bertha to come by. It just doesn't matter to me whether my company is $1 million, $10 million, or $1 billion. The important questions to me are; is my business profitable, am I creating personal wealth, and am I leading the life I want to lead? My answer to all three questions is, "Yes." So, why would I want to grow my company just for the sake of growth, and risk changing all that?

I have not had the opportunity to run a larger company. I realize my management job would change if I grew my company and it reached sales of over, say, $20 million. The prospect of running a company that large, however, doesn't scare me at all. Owners should start a company with the idea of becoming a solidly successful business that makes money at low volume levels. Don't plan from the beginning on building a company that must become large in order to survive. It's much better to structure a new business to make money from the beginning, and then keep the profits rolling year after year. I know how to do that. That's basic. That's how I stay in control. The next steps don't frighten me. If I ever got the urge to grow, I know I could do it because I know how to make money in a small business.

But I keep reminding myself that volume is just volume. By itself, it does not create profitability or wealth. Look at all the ego-driven, growth-oriented companies that end up in the dump. During the 1980s, it seemed that everyone was into gross volume. Volume by itself means absolutely nothing. Solid success—year after year—means something to me.

It's certainly not chiseled in stone that a company must grow continuously in order to survive. To survive and prosper, owners must create solidly-positioned, money-making machines, and this can be accomplished with limited or no growth. We don't need more bigness for the sake of bigness. America needs lean, profitable companies, large and small, that are continuously profitable and liquid in any economic climate. Solid, stable companies of the right size have a much better shot at survival and steady prosperity than the "go-go" set. "Go-go" companies may produce more jobs on the way up, but those jobs disappear quickly on the way back down.

But how can growth possibly hurt you, Roy?

If an owner does feel an uncontrollable urge to grow, my advice is, "Beware!" Poorly executed growth kills more companies than virtually any other reason. The newspapers are full of examples. Don't let raw ambition cloud your common sense and perspective. If you play your cards right, you can achieve extraordinary personal aggrandizement owning a well-run, small, steady, solid and profitable business.

I'm glad that Southwest Apparel is a small company, and it's likely to remain that way. More ambitious owners may grow their companies to a larger size than my company, but growth sucks up cash. They may not have enough cash in the till to weather a storm, and a storm is bound to come along, sooner or later.

Many companies in the garment industry made big mistakes when they put themselves into a rapid growth mode. They ran into people and management problems immediately. Overhead got completely out of line. The owner who started the company found he could visit his new plants only once a month instead of weekly. He lost control over operations. It was difficult to find the kind of people that could become dependable plant managers. As soon as a glitch occurred, they were history.

Everyone seems to want to grow at 10% a year, but life isn't like that. Maybe you could as easily lose 10% a year, or better yet, you could continue doing the same volume and be even more profitable. The key factors are profitability and cash flow. If you can produce profitability, positive cash flow and continuous liquidity, and also have growth at the same time, that's fine. Many have tried. Few have succeeded.

Uncontrolled growth, or even rapid, controlled growth plays havoc with positive cash flow. It consumes huge amounts of working capital by forcing receivables and inventories to grow. If you're not prepared financially, you can grow yourself right into a cash crunch.

An owner can lose a business by trying to be more profitable through forced growth, or lose it for sure by not being profitable at all. Growth is an "everything" problem. Growth is many-faceted. If you don't predict and handle properly every single bend in the road, you can lose your company quickly. Just because your business has surplus cash available doesn't necessarily mean you can grow with safety. People lose sight of that. Anything can happen. A quality problem might develop, or personnel problems could cut into productivity. In fact, large infusions of cash have created terrible company problems because they encourage increases in staff or erosion of quality or productivity due to the complacency that results from a fat bank account. It happens all the time. It's much better to bootstrap a business from the beginning and be profitable from day one. To do that, *slow, orderly growth is a must.*

When companies grow beyond a certain point, that wonderful, close relationship the owners have with their management teams begins to fall apart. No longer can the owner get away with the quick conferences in the hall and the phone-call meetings. Suddenly, you feel compelled to expand your staff and add overhead. You'll be sitting in your office and communicating more formally—dealing with procedures, planning sessions, management meetings, reports—all that professional management bull that comes with large, complex organizations. It's a whole new ball game, and a damned expensive and risky one. Size alone doesn't necessarily make a business more effective or efficient. It's usually the other way around.

Some owners may feel obliged to work hard on increasing market share. Their obsession with market share tempts them to grow beyond their means, and that's very risky. It's better, instead, to forget about market share and focus on what it's going to take to satisfy your own needs and goals. Find the right risk-reward relationship for yourself, and for your company—and go for it.

When advisors encourage you to grow, *consider the sources and their motives.* They may be primarily interested in making money by taking the business public or arranging other financing, or from trading in your stock. Even conventional bankers can lead you down the primrose path of growth if they can cover their risks through an SBA-guaranteed loan or loan covenants that you would be crazy to accept. The "money boys," like accountants, lawyers, bankers and stockbrokers, hope they'll make money on your growth. Be wary of them when they encourage you to enter a risky growth venture. Remember that your advisors don't take the risks. You do!

If a new customer were to call me tomorrow and offer to give me a $10 million order—more than doubling my company's size, I'd consider it, but I would be extremely reluctant to charge ahead without giving it some very careful thought. One big danger of rapid growth like this is that the new business may only be viable for a shorter time than I anticipate. I would need to tally up all the incremental costs and investments that would be required to support the business, including people and additional equipment, and see if the resulting profits are worth the risk. If the project falls short of expectations, I may end up with horrendous carrying charges that won't go away. That could really drag me down and kill what I have already achieved. Growth can quickly become an owner's worst enemy. It's Murphy's Law . . . if something can go wrong, it will. Growth is full of traps.

A well run business shouldn't have to do $20 million in sales to earn a million in profits for its owner. I don't know about you, but I'd be satisfied with $1 million in profits each year on $5 million in sales, especially if it's all mine. Why should I take the risks of being a larger player when I can get what I need out of life with a safe, stable level of sales?

When has a company reached the "right" size, Roy?

The way I look at it, the "right" size for a company is the sales volume at which it can achieve and maintain extraordinary productivity and profitability. Figuring out just what that size is is one of an owner's toughest jobs. Determining at what sales level you can get the *most out for the least in—with minimum risk*, that's what responsible management is all about.

We've all heard business owners complain that they made more money at $5 million in sales than they are now making at $20 million. I call this common phenomenon the "Progressive Paralysis Syndrome." It happens when the owner gets dissatisfied with the "lousy" $500,000 profit he is making at $5 million in sales, and gets an uncontrollable urge to go for big time profits at $20 million. The owner thinks things are going to get a lot better, but they don't. Things usually get progressively worse with growth beyond a particular level of sales. Don't assume growth somehow always equates to greater profits. Sorry, it just doesn't.

What often happens is that owners are able to get by with virtually no overhead at $5 million in sales when they don't know any better. Then their advisors tell them they need all that extra "stuff" that's required to be a "success" at $20 million. Well, all that "stuff" is what increases their operating expenses from 6% of sales to 14% of sales. Guess what happens to profits? They'll be lucky if their profits stay flat at $20 million in sales. Often, they go down.

Fortunately, there's a way to beat this syndrome. You do it by insisting on slow and orderly growth to the "right" level of sales and organization, a level where a company can optimize its results compared to its costs and risks. You need to figure out what level of cash generation is necessary to maintain a profitable business in your industry, while also allowing a satisfactory level of wealth creation for yourself. That's the "right" level. Make sure you're achieving that level of cash generation now, or focus your attention on building towards that level in the immediate future.

The "right" size for your company provides a steady

stream of sales and profits, assures continuous liquidity, and allows a desirable life-style for the owner, in good times as well as bad. At that level, your business will be able to respond to market down-turns while maintaining profitability and cash flow. Of course, you have to select and size all elements of cost carefully so you can shrink easily in reaction to lower levels of business. Then you can have solid profitability in the best of times, and better yet—in the worst of times.

Let's say the "right" sales level for your company is $6 million. Trying to grow your business to $15 million could be just so much overkill, or, worse luck, it could kill your company. There's a tremendous difference between running a $6 million business and a $15 million business. Growth beyond the "right" size increases the complexity of the business and cuts into your safety margins. If you hold your business at the highly profitable $6 million level, you'll be in a stronger position to deal with the glitches that are bound to occur. If you're making enough money to satisfy your personal goals at $6 million, why not stop right there? Continued growth beyond the "right" size may only increase your risks without offsetting rewards.

Of course, a start-up company has to get to the elusive "right" level in the first place, so some growth is required for any new business. When you reach the level where you're achieving your personal goals, stop growing. Work on strengthening your company's market position and on improving its ability to reward you handsomely. Forget the "go-go" growth promoters. Make money your way. You'll lose no points in heaven by staying small, profitable, and solid, *very solid*. You may even gain a few points.

How, then, should an owner control growth?

Even during the recession when all the downsizing and adjusting was going on, I had an awful feeling that many companies, large and small, were still missing the point. Something seemed to be telling their chief executives in the back of their heads that if they weren't growing, they were failing. Many "experts" still encourage this false thinking. The treadmill philosophy, where you feel you have to grow continually year after year, is nonsense. Businesses have to produce a successful product and make a profit. And if you own the company, you want to create some wealth along the way. Pure volume or growth has nothing to do with accomplishing your goals. You have to run your company right, and that means orderly growth, or maybe no growth at all.

The woods are full of examples of disorderly growth. Today you can't pick up any newspaper without learning more than you want to know about how the excessive use of debt and unrestrained growth have caused the demise of former "hot shot" companies. Don't follow their examples. You don't need their grief.

As I've said, a basic rule for achieving solid success is: *Limit all investments and expenditures to the availability of operating cash flow.* If you follow this rule, you'll have a much better chance for continuous profits and positive cash flow, with or without growth. This rule should become your "Board of Directors"—your "strategic plan." It gets back to my conviction that your business is your plan. You're in control. You can run your business this way if you want to.

Of course, you can always go to your advisors and they'll show you that if you raise a few million bucks, you can end up with fifty restaurants instead of your present one successful eatery. It all sounds great, but the odds are in favor of your joining the trash heap of history. You might very well end up taking on too much debt in order to feed the growth beast. When you're planning for aggressive growth, you can make your spreadsheet projections come out anyway you want. Unfortunately, they probably don't reflect reality, so you could be in for a painful surprise.

Never get into a situation where you must increase your size just to stay alive and continue your bank line. That's a lot like a pyramid scheme. Get your company into a situation where there's enough working capital to sustain operations even in downturns—a situation in which you can have authority and autonomy. Be in a position to self-finance the business. Be able to say "no" to a product that won't make you money right away. Loss leaders are just drills. You don't need drills. Let someone else do the drills.

What's wrong with doing business the old-fashioned way—financing growth through earnings, building a profitable company and acquiring personal wealth through company profits? Profits get translated eventually into retained earnings and working capital if you're running your company right. Growth that is limited by operating cash flow usually means slow growth. What's wrong with that? If you're already achieving your personal goals from the business, why even think about fast growth?

This is why it makes sense to finance just about everything a smaller company wants and needs through the cash generated from operating cash flow. I understand that everybody needs a working capital credit line to help finance seasonal working capital needs. But every other need for funds, *especially* funds required to finance growth in sales volume, should come from accumulated operating cash flow. This includes buying the equipment needed to produce the increased business, and even the incremental receivables and inventory that will get your company up to a new, higher level of business. Once there, you can fall back on your regular credit line for seasonal working capital needs.

By using operating cash flow as an owner's guide to orderly growth, you have a much better chance of achieving your personal goals of building a solid company, accumulating some wealth, being your own boss, and leading a balanced life. If a burning need to grow develops before enough cash is available to finance the expansion internally, *wait!* Gradually build up the company's internal financing capability, and then make your move. Most opportunities can be made to wait. Don't bite off more than you can chew!

I keep my business at a level that's right for me, and on a steady, even keel. As a result, I sleep very well at night. I make all the money and create all the wealth that any reasonable person could want. What more could anyone ask?

What about starting an additional business?

I know many successful business owners who have become bored by their original successes after a few years. They start thinking of themselves as some sort of conglomerate gurus. "I made ABC work for me, didn't I? So, why don't I start another business and get the creative juices flowing again?" With that kind of thinking, we're talking about major risk, and I mean *major risk.* If you're really and truly bored with your success, the best approach is to sell the first business, and put all your energies into the new business. That will work. But if you fancy your company becoming a multi-division company, you could be heading for trouble.

One basic rule applies in this situation. Never screw with your money source. I'll repeat that—*never screw with your money source!* If you have a company that works and is making money for you, don't even think about using the cash flow of that first business to pay for growing a new business. And never allow the second business to be at the mercy of the first, and vice versa. If you feel you must start that second business, keep both businesses self-contained. Don't screw with your money source! If you do, your whole deck of cards might just come tumbling down.

Wealthy families in America control profitable businesses that keep generating income. Life-styles are maintained and trusts are funded. They don't mess with a major chunk of their principal and plunk it down on new, high-flyer bets. They don't mess with the basic source of their wealth.

If you want to take a flyer, however, decide how much money you want to risk, take the risk, and don't be terribly surprised if you lose it all. A few years ago, I bought into an apartment building, a movie, an oil well and a gas well, hoping to broaden my business interests. None of them worked out. Because of that experience, I no longer take flyers. I'm a quick study. It was an expensive education for me. Now, I stick with my money source, Southwest Apparel, and I don't even consider messing with it. That's why it's so solid. I stick to my knitting.

During recent years, many owners thought that unbridled growth was the only strategy for success. As a result, they didn't generate any real money, and they didn't create solid, profitable, steady results. Many ended up in the dump. I'm a bone fide businessman. I make a product that actually gets consumed by real people. I don't need to be a growth star to enjoy solid success.

Basically, you prefer responsible, orderly, profitable operations to growth. Right?

Right! I don't get hung up by thinking like stock

market people think, where growth is king. I do what's right for me—what makes it possible for me to achieve my personal goals. I don't live with the illusion that growth is somehow going to help me reach my goals or solve all my problems. Many companies still think it's a good idea to take their profits and grow the business to gain more market clout. A baby food company tried that recently. They were doing very well making baby food, but then they thought they would grow into the diaper business. I guess they wanted to cash in on the other end of the action. But the diaper business didn't do as well as they hoped, so many diaper workers lost their jobs. That's not responsible management, and it certainly isn't orderly growth.

I've been talking about the orderly growth of a company to the "right" size where its owner can enjoy exceptional cash generation and profitability, a strong market position, and, ultimately, solid success. A basic requirement to pull that off? *Be very, very, very wary of growth!*

The Quick-Study Guide
for Independent Business Owners

BE VERY WARY OF GROWTH

- Make money from day one. Don't be forced to grow to make money.
- Volume is just volume. It does not, by itself, create profitability or wealth.
- A company can survive and prosper without continuous growth.
- If they are run right, smaller companies can become big profit producers.
- Growth affects everything. Think carefully about all possible "land mines" before launching any growth program.
- Grow your business to the "right" size—the size that meets your personal goals and produces a stable business in your industry. Then slow down growth, or stop growing altogether.
- Make the availability of funds from operating cash flow be your guide and limit when considering any new project, including growth.
- Positive cash flow is the ultimate success factor, not growth.
- Pushing for market share risks unsound growth.
- Beware of the "Progressive Paralysis Syndrome." Growth can reduce profitability and overall productivity.
- The "right" sized business can survive market downturns with continued profitability and liquidity.
- For solidly successful results, focus on profitability, positive cash flow, and serving your customers better, rather than on growth.

13

ROY'S RULE NO. 12:

Be Happy!

LIVING A BALANCED AND FULFILLING LIFE

Business is supposed to be fun. If it isn't, you're doing something wrong. If it is, you're making your company work for you, providing you with the time and resources you can devote to a complete and balanced family and personal life beyond the base business. Business owners who live balanced lives make better business owners.

What priority does business have in your life, Roy?

For me, happiness comes from living a balanced life. Having a balanced life is what gets me up in the morning, eager to take on the world. I make a point of balancing the time I spend appropriately among my business, my family and the fun interests I have outside my business. I work hard at all three, but I know which comes first. Above all, my family comes first—before my business and my outside activities. When something needs to get done to make my business a success, however, it gets my undivided attention, because a successful business is what allows me to be close to my family and do all the other things I want to do with my life.

On a strictly personal basis, business cannot and will not be my whole life. I do have other interests, and I'm not at all ashamed of pursuing them. In fact, I'm proud of them. They help make me a more complete person. There are roses, and roses, and roses out there. I can see them. By God, I'm going to smell them, too!

I realize I have to do whatever it takes to get the job done, but I have structured my business so that I don't have to spend all my available time on work. I could. I could spend most of my time doing my job. But I would miss out on the other aspects of my life—all the other things I love to do. The other activities help me be a better owner, and they're fun. Damn it! *Life is supposed to be fun!*

I'm having a great life. I'm a happy guy. The only thing we humans run out of is time. I have enough self-confidence and raw intelligence to know that I should be able to achieve success in business and in life. But there are many ways to measure success. For me, success means always being able to do what I want, when I want to do it. That doesn't mean that I can get away with shunning my business responsibilities.

I like to be friendly with my customers and get to know business people in my industry and in other industries. I try to socialize with business associates after work, because I enjoy talking about business in a social setting. I even enjoy transacting business, because I really enjoy working. You've got it. *Business is also supposed to be fun!*

Does this sound somehow irresponsible, or too free-spirited? I would hate to see the free spirit taken out of Americans. The epitome of free spirit is in our entrepreneurs, and I feel like I'm one of them. To be a free-spirited entrepreneur, one has to come to terms with the work ethic of most Americans. This whole "work-ethic" thing has gotten bandied around so much lately. It's as if work should be the be-all and end-all of everyone's existence. To be a success in business as well as in life, in my opinion, is not a matter of just working more hours. We all know that in life as in sex, length is not everything. There's more to life and business success than just putting in long hours at the office.

It takes all kinds of people to run successful businesses, but I don't want to be like just anybody. I want to live my life *my* way. I want to be in charge of my life, and not be a slave to my business. I'll be damned if I'm going to have a defined work schedule. If other owners run their businesses the right way, they can also lead a great life beyond their commitments to their base businesses.

Where do you think you fit into the full spectrum of business owners, Roy?

Nothing is fair in life, and that holds true for business, too. There are always the extremes. Some chief executives get paid a ton of money, and they do little to deserve it. Other people work their asses off, do a good job, and don't have anything to show for it. That's life.

Not everyone aspires to the kind of life I choose to lead. Other owners don't need to live life my way to be a success in business. But if they do, it sure doesn't hurt either them or their businesses. Look at all the business owners you know who might just as well be married to their businesses. They spend most of their waking hours pushing their companies to some idealized level of performance that they are literally dying to achieve but never seem to reach. I guess if the situation is better at the office than it is at home, I could understand why people would spend so much time at the office. Or if the situation is better out on the road, I could also understand why on owner would want to spend a lot of time traveling. To me, that's not what life is all about.

Many owners are really convinced they must work twelve hours a day to succeed. They feel guilty if they aren't putting in man-killing hours. The point is that putting time in at one end doesn't necessarily produce success at the other end. Spending lots of hours at something doesn't necessarily make someone good at it. It might even mean the opposite. Maybe you're not running your business right. Maybe you're not organized right. Maybe you're doing things that a solidly successful business owner should not be spending much time doing. You might need to think more about what you are doing, and what you are asking other people to do. This could change you from being a slave to your business, to being a happy, fulfilled person.

Simply put, I want to be a successful business person *and* have a great, balanced life, but I insist on doing both at the same time. Is that impossible? I don't think so. Is this desire somehow sinful or irresponsible? Not when my family, my customers and my employees are being well served. Does my happy, balanced life keep me from running a successful business? No way! *That's what makes me solidly successful!*

Roy, how do you structure your business and personal interests so they work so well together?

I decided a long time ago that it wasn't all that important for me to conquer the whole world. Part of it, maybe, but not the whole tamale. Personally, I have lots of other interests besides my business—things I like to do. I've been lucky and successful enough to make enough money so I can do what I want, when I want to do it, and run a solid company in between. I don't need the corporate jet, but I do book a first class ticket when I fly to see a customer. That's a great way to meet interesting people. But, I always try to have some weekdays free to pursue my outside interests. It's not enough to just devote weekends to the fun things in life. I don't like to schedule recreational activities only on weekends. Vail is too crowded on weekends. The ski lift lines are too long. Life is too short for that!

I do enjoy spending time with my family. We participate in all sorts of things together, like going on family outings outside the state when everybody else is coming to Arizona to soak up the rays. I have many other interests outside of my business. My wife and I enjoy our community. We even support the few politicians we happen to respect and like. And I get a huge kick out of meeting interesting people. They're the spice of life, because they have so much to offer me.

Somewhere along the line, many business owners have lost sight of what it's all about—running a successful operation. We're not supposed to be the guys who are hoisting up the blocks for the pyramids. We're supposed to be the guys who commissioned the pyramids. Where does it say an owner has to spend fourteen hours a day on the business to be successful? What about your family? What about your happiness?

My personal obsession is to be very efficient at what I do, and then realize the possible drawbacks of maybe not going to the factory every week, or not getting on the road every Sunday night and coming back Friday night. I just find a way to make it work. I work hard on structuring my life, my company and everything else I do so I can live the life I'm determined to live.

When I structure my work habits properly, I find I'm able to spend a significant portion of my time on other activities that interest me. Coming into a garment buying season, my business may take full days of my time. Fine. But when the rush is over, in a month or two, and it takes zero hours a day to run the business, it's over! If I'm well-organized and I'm very productive with the use of my time, I can live a balanced life and not hurt the success of Southwest Apparel one penny's worth.

People ask me where I spend my time. It's hard to put percentages on the time I spend running the business and doing what I want to do beyond the business. Every week is different. Typically, though, I might spend half my time dealing with customers and other external business activities, twenty percent on monitoring the factory's operations and the flow of cash, and the rest of my waking hours on interesting outside activities. This schedule gives me plenty of time for spending part of every week with my family and on fun. Except during busy seasons. Then it's time to work!.

Running a successful business requires that the owner get a huge number of tasks done right. Either the owner must do them, or the owner needs to get someone else to do them. My operations manager has full charge of everything that goes on at the plant—the "internals." Having given him that responsibility and having full trust in what he's doing, I stay out of his operations—except for oversight, of course.

I spend my time where I know that I excel and where I can really make a difference in the success of the company. For me that means working on the "externals," mainly sales, customer development, product definition, marketing and finance. There's no need for me to be at the factory to do this, so having my home twelve hundred miles away from the shop works out fine. I speak with the factory managers every day on the phone from my home office in Phoenix, or from the road. I monitor operations and shipments, and keep a close watch over cash flow. But the point is, I don't waste time accomplishing the tasks I have assigned to myself to do. I get in there, get it done, and then go on to other things. I try to keep everything simple, so the managers and I don't waste time stumbling over each other. And I make a big point not to spend any time at all on things that are not directly related to making money for the company.

I tell my factory people that if a problem occurs, I'm available to help, any time, any place. But I'm not available just to hang around the shop in hopes that someone will need me. I'd rather be doing other things, like living a balanced life.

Again, permit me to be blunt. I have no intention of working eighty-hour weeks. I'm just not going to do it! I can't imagine why anyone would willingly put up with that. I feel I should be able to get my work done in no more than eight hours a day, even during the busy season. If I can't get it done in eight hours, I feel that instead of me out-smarting the system, the system is out-smarting me, and that's a personal affront to my intelligence. If it takes me more than eight hours, I know that I'm not working as smart as I can, and I change something I'm doing that's dumb. Of course, other owners may feel they have to put in unbelievable hours just to make their businesses work. Owners can make a *real job* out of running a business if they let it happen. Heaven forbid!

The owner of a Southwest Apparel supplier called me one night from New York at 9 o'clock, his time. I said, "Phil, what's the deal? Did the plant burn down? Why are you calling me so late?" He said, "I'm usually here every day from 7 am to at least 7 pm" I said, "I can't do that, Phil. I'm just not going to do that!" Phil replied, "You know, I talk to many company presidents who run companies like mine. They tell me the hours they put in are unbelievable. Seventy to eighty hours a week." Then Phil said something that hit me between the eyes. He said, "That's what it takes today to get the job done."

You're wrong, Phil. You are dead wrong. If you can't find a way to live a balanced life and have a little fun with your business, something is terribly wrong with what you are doing, and how you are doing it. Change something. It just doesn't have to be that way.

How would you advise other owners to decide on the right balance between work and a full life?

Owners need to decide what the right balance is for them between the business itself, the family, and all the other interests that add spice to their lives. I can't really say what the perfect mix is. Some very successful business owners are all "profit" and no "pleasure." Everybody is different. Personally, I know what I want my mix to be. I just make sure that it works out that way. If you're running your company the way it ought to be run, you should have plenty of time on your hands to lead a wonderful life beyond your base business. Your business is your path to happiness.

If you want all the entrapments of a business, like getting people to call you up and take you out to lunch—fine. I personally don't care about those things. To me, it's not the six speakers in the car, lunch at the club every day, and the fancy office on the top floor of the office building that counts. What counts for me is building a solidly successful company and having enough control over events to live a balanced and fulfilling life.

Roy, what do owners have to do to lead great lives beyond their businesses?

First of all, the owner has to be a producer, not just a manager. You've got to be at the helm and in total charge, all the time. If you have the right resources working for you, you can do away with a lot of the details that most owners get involved with—those non-productive things that suck up so much of their time. Your primary job is to get out into the marketplace, create an opportunity, get an order, and make arrangements to have it made and shipped and the money collected. That's the name of the game. That's all there is to it! When you've done that, free time should be left over for the pursuit of happiness.

It's critical, though, that you separate the company's direction-setting activities from the day-to-day operations of the business. Set the company's direction and work the "externals" yourself. Find an excellent operations manager who is fully capable of running the day-to-day "internals." Then stay in daily contact with that manager, no matter where you might be at the time. Monitor what's happening daily, but don't even think about taking over any part of the operations manager's job, once he has proven himself.

Also, owners may need to sharpen up their own work habits. We all get a little dull. The trick is to get in there, and get your work done fast. Work like a beaver when something needs to get done. When the work level slackens, don't feel guilty about not hanging around the plant to "show the flag" to your troops. If the right relationships and responsibilities with your management team are in place, they'll do a great job without your being present every moment of the time.

When "free" time occurs, make a point of leaving your office or the plant, and go off with your family or in pursuit of your other interests. Do the things that bring your life into balance and make you a whole person. Don't feel guilty. Get away from the shop!

You also might try living where you want to live. Modern communications and technology being what they are, it's no longer necessary for an owner to live right next to the plant or office. Make use of the telephone, computers, modems, faxes, express package delivery, airplanes—all the technology-based management tools that help you be productive and in control wherever you happen to be. With technology, you can be visiting clients a thousand miles from home base or hitting the slopes at Vail and still be in total control of your business. Let's face it! You can live anywhere you want to these days—anyplace where a balanced life really works for you.

How does a balanced life help you and your business?

I feel very strongly that business owners need to have life-broadening experiences that are outside of their narrow business endeavors. There's no reason why an owner shouldn't spend a little time in the search for beauty, and a lot of time with family and friends. That means getting out into the world and becoming part of the world. Don't become isolated within your industry where you can become completely unbalanced. Don't let yourself be insulated from what's going on in the rest of the world.

Outside experiences provide owners with a continuing stream of great ideas that they may want to apply to their businesses. These experiences keep you in touch with reality—the real world. If you schedule your business life so you can do this, you'll inevitably do a better job running your company. You'll get useful ideas for your business from people who aren't in your industry at all.

That's one reason why I have never been a big fan of trade associations. I have no desire to be the big guy at the trade association meeting. If that's important to the people who work for me, they can belong to the trade association. I'd rather spend my time with a guy who can show me how he catches butterflies and mounts them on a piece of glass. It's more interesting, and, who knows, there may be something there that applies to how I put tickets on garments. Only thinking and talking about my own business is a dull way to live a life. It's not for me.

We're all looking for ingenious ideas that will help our businesses become more successful. But the question is, does ingenuity come from within, or from without? For me, ingenuity is an external thing. It comes from influences and contacts that are outside of my daily environment, and usually outside of my business.

The ideas I get from the outside world feed me and give me new insights. They have helped my company become solidly successful. Am I just engaging in rationalization? I don't think so. Southwest Apparel is successful, and I'm having a lot of fun. It works for me.

What's the ultimate payoff from living a balanced and fulfilling life?

Business owners shouldn't feel guilty if they're not at the office on Saturday and holidays. Many of these "80-hour-a-week" types are probably taking it upon themselves to work the "internals," acting more like operations managers than owners or chief executives. "Internal" activities are constant, and they happen at the factory or the office, not out in the marketplace. Many owners operate this way, and in some cases it works for them. You can certainly work the "internals" if you want to, but it's a tough life and very time consuming. You risk not being on top of the "externals," and that's where the solid success of your business really comes from. By concentrating on the "externals," owners can enjoy the flexibility to do what they want to do, when they want to do it, and to live full and balanced lives while running solidly successful companies.

The basic business beliefs I have been talking about—an owner's guidelines for solid business success—are just one way to run a successful company. There are other ways to skin the same cat. There are the dedicated owners who do the twelve hours a day, six days a week routine. Not much time with the family, of course, or for other outside interests. That doesn't mean that they can't be "successful" as they interpret the word.

That kind of a life is not for me. I hope I've been able to show that it just doesn't have to be that way for a business owner to become solidly successful. *Lighten up! Be happy! Take some time to smell those roses!* You and your company will be a whole lot better off for it!

The Quick-Study Guide for Independent Business Owners

BE HAPPY!

• Having a solidly successful business is what gives an owner the opportunity to live a balanced life and pursue happiness.

• Having a balanced life means spending quality time with family and friends and enjoying personal interests while running a successful business.

• Solidly successful owners are able to do what they want to do, when they want to do it.

• Business owners benefit from having other experiences beyond their basic work experience.

• Get out into the world. Don't become a captive of your business and industry. Gaining outside perspectives helps owners run better companies.

• If you are running your company right and making use of Roy's Rules, you should have plenty of time to pursue outside interests.

• If you don't have time to pursue outside interests, you are doing something wrong. Find out what it is, and change it!

• With a good "operations manager" to run the "internals," you will find time to work the "externals" while leading a balanced life.

• You must work hard at structuring your business, your role in it, and your outside interests in order to lead a balanced life.

• Never feel guilty about not working 80-hour weeks, or not working on Saturdays. Lighten up! Be happy! Business is supposed to be fun!

14

On to Solid Success!

There you have them. Roy's Rules. Roy Jacobson's twelve basic business beliefs—his guiding principles, core management philosophies and mental disciplines—that have led to solid success for this extraordinary business owner. A picture of a dedicated entrepreneur at work producing outstanding results for his company and in his life has emerged from our conversation. It's an impressive picture, the envy of most business owner.

You are probably now asking yourself, "If I operate my business according to Roy's Rules, can I expect the same results?" You have probably discovered that some of Roy's Rules are already playing an important role in how you run your business, while others may sound a bit too "different" for you. Before you step off the plank and adopt all of Roy's Rules, let's look at the driving forces that Roy has applied to get to the head of the class.

Forces that drive Roy's
extraordinary results

The three forces that have kept Roy and his business on track, moving steadily and purposefully toward achieving solid success in his business and his life, are (1) his personal goals, (2) his focus on one overriding business objective, and (3) the twelve principles that guide all of his business decisions, Roy's Rules.

Roy's personal goals are simple. He wants to create a continuous stream of wealth, be in total control of his life, and pursue happiness for himself and for others who are important to him, especially his family. Roy keeps these personal goals clearly in front of him all the time. He simply does not allow anyone or anything to interfere with their accomplishment. If a business activity or strategy does not completely support his personal goals, he changes it, or drops it altogether.

Roy's one overriding business objective is to focus all business activities exclusively on the key factors that are truly important to solid success. He refuses to waste a single ounce of his own or his company's energy and resources on any business activity or strategy that does not contribute directly and immediately to making money and keeping customers satisfied. Roy's thoughts and actions are driven by his obsession to produce outstanding products and services, to be close to his customers and markets, and to remain the lowest cost producer in his segment of the apparel industry. That's what is truly important to Roy. As he says, "Everything else is just so much excess baggage."

Roy's Rules guide every move Roy makes. He continually applies the twelve basic business beliefs we have reviewed as a framework and test for decision-making. These fundamental management philosophies are at the core of Roy's being, and they have contributed in a major way to Roy's solid success. Upon them rest the ultimate success and stability of his company and his ability to achieve his personal goals. His management principles work their way into all aspects of his business and personal life—how and where he spends his time, how he deals with customers, how he relates to his management team, how he controls costs and maximizes profitability—everything!

All owners possess basic business beliefs, their own set of management philosophies and principles which may or may not help them reach solid success. What's the fundamental lesson to be learned from Roy's success? *The ability of independent business owners to convert their management principles and business beliefs into operational realities determines, for better or for worse, how well their companies perform and how likely they are to reach their personal goals through their businesses.* This means that all business owners would be well advised to challenge their own management principles and basic business beliefs to see how well they really contribute to achieving their personal and business goals. Some of their principles and beliefs just may not help!

Applying Roy's Rules has certainly helped Roy Jacobson produce exceptional results in his business, and even in his personal life outside of his business. Applying Roy's Rules in day-to-day decision-making may help other independent business owners achieve their personal goals while attaining solid financial and operational success for their businesses.

Applying Roy's Rules

The decision of any independent business owner to adopt—or not to adopt—Roy's Rules for the benefit of the owner's company and life can be boiled down to this. If the path you are now following in running your business lacks a clear commitment to solid success as we have defined the term, or if you are obsessed primarily with survival, you had better get used to the idea of never achieving anything more satisfying than "ho-hum" results. If, on the other hand, you are grimly determined to follow the path of rapid growth, trying to transform your independent company into a large, impressive corporate showpiece, you can certainly do that, given sufficient capital and management resources. But, beware—that path can be very risky, and the risk is mainly yours. The trade-offs you may suffer can become excruciating—too little time with family and friends, a risk-reward relationship that is heavily skewed towards risk, and a lack of total control over your life.

You may very well find, instead, that your personal objectives can be more certainly reached by following a third path. That path follows Roy's Rules to solid success—a path that may well include slow growth or no growth, lowest possible costs, great customers, bona fide receivables, little or no long-term debt and exceptional profits.

Roy Jacobson has demonstrated how following Roy's Rules can lead to solid success for one independent business owner. Every business owner, however, has different capabilities and goals. Every business is different. Before adopting Roy's Rules, you should recognize that Roy's management philosophies can and should be adapted to your personality, your goals, your industry and your specific business environment in order to make them work right for you. With a little thought, you can adapt each of Roy's Rules to your own situation, integrating them with your existing management philosophies— those with which you are already comfortable, and those that brought you through the start-up battles to where you are today.

Start-up entrepreneurs will be interested in noting that Roy's Rules are just as applicable when applied at the beginning of a company as they are at its prime. If you are contemplating taking the plunge into entrepreneurship, you may find that following Roy's Rules from the start will enhance your new company's chances of reaching puberty, and maybe even a ripe old age. This is particularly true for the many refugees from major corporation downsizings who are launching new enterprises of their own. Following the "rules" learned at major corporate institutions when starting a new company can be the kiss of death. New rules apply. If this is your lot, you'd better study up fast on Roy's Rules!

Roy's company, of course, is a small manufacturer in the apparel industry. Business owners in other manufacturing industries, and also in retail, distribution and services industries, will find that many of the basic management principles that are expressed by Roy's Rules are equally applicable in their industries, though they may need to be interpreted to fit the context of specific competitive environments. Take the variables into consideration in adapting Roy's Rules to your company, particularly your location, the specific types of products or services you offer, the peculiarities of your industry, the type of labor force you have and need, the forms of financing available to you, and the level of technology required by your business.

If you happen to work for a large, complex corporation, you will find that Roy's Rules can even be applied to the horrendous management problems often found in your domain. The basic business units—the divisions— of your company can be run much like solidly successful, independent businesses if the division general managers of your company are given the latitude and incentives to run their business entities as Roy Jacobson operates his small manufacturing business. The scales may be different, but most of the management principles and disciplines required for the "chief operator" of a division to become solidly successful are the same. Roy's Rules have a role to play at Gargantuan Industries!

No matter what your industry or the size of your company, putting Roy's Rules to work in your life and in your business can move you towards solid success, and the personal benefits and contributions to life itself that can be derived from becoming solidly successful are monumental. You can find the time to be much closer to your family than most business owners. The wealth your business creates can give you the opportunity to engage in outside pursuits that interest you. You can reward your key management team handsomely. You can support the economic health of the communities in which your workers live. You can contribute to the nation's bank of solid companies that compete successfully in the global economy and that provide steady employment, good wages and excellent working conditions for their wonderful American workers. A challenging journey, but one well worth the effort.

Creating solid success

Most business owners work very hard for solid success, and they shouldn't settle for anything less. Before you assume, however, that the ultimate reward—solid success—is yours for the taking, be aware of this most fundamental of truths. Your ability to enjoy a wonderful, balanced life is *completely dependent* on the ability of your company to experience extraordinary financial success, becoming a solid wealth-creator, year after year. The good things you want to do in life can be yours when the profits are there, and *only when they are there*—now and in the future. The lesson? *Concentrate on financial success first. Personal success and a wonderful life can follow.*

The first vital step for an owner to take on the journey towards solid success is to fully embrace your own adaptations of Roy's Rules. Translating Roy's basic beliefs into meaningful and reliable management action, however, requires that an owner put operating practices into place that are compatible with and supportive of Roy's Rules. Roy's specific operating practices that have been described above may stimulate your thoughts on developing improved operating practices for yourself and your company—such practices as the management roles you play as owner, how you operate with minimum overhead, and the degree to which you make investment decisions based on the availability of operating cash flow. Do this, and you will have created the foundation of a solid success that lasts.

What has Roy really accomplished?

Roy Jacobson has achieved every one of the personal goals he set for himself when he started Southwest Apparel. He enjoys a high level of income, and he has been able to set aside enough personal assets to assure his family's financial security. His business is steadily profitable, year after year. Roy has a high degree of control over his life—much more so than most business owners. I can attest to the fact that "happiness" is there. He really enjoys his business and the wonderful, balanced life that it enables him to pursue.

Beyond achieving his personal goals, Roy has the deep satisfaction of living a contained, orderly, sensible life. He refuses to be part of the "go-go" mentality that thinks going public, building paper profits, taking home unearned bonuses, and thrashing the company into fast growth is the only way for an exemplary business owner to behave. He knows that he has built a solid, cash-producing machine that benefits its customers, its suppliers, its employees and the communities in which it operates. He lusts for nothing more.

Is Roy taking too much out of his business in order to support his enviable lifestyle? Of course not. His extraordinarily low overhead costs, high earnings and continuing cash flow are the very accomplishments that keep him from succumbing to pressures to scrimp on wages and bonuses for productive employees. High-overhead companies are all too susceptible to those pressures. In fact, Roy can afford to pay good wages, provide supportive working conditions and, best of all, keep his productive employees on the job through thick and thin—and he does.

Roy works very hard at keeping a steady flow of production in his plants. Many of Roy's competitors repeatedly lay off excess operators, and then hire others back later as production levels swing widely from season to season. Roy keeps his production force quite level from season to season, and from year to year. Steady production means steady employment for his workers.

These accomplishments have resulted in exemplary employment security for the workers of Southwest Apparel. That high degree of employment security is best achieved when an independent company is managed in accordance with Roy's Rules—when a company is solidly successful. Roy wouldn't have it any other way.

Roy Jacobson would never admit to it, but he has every right to be satisfied and thankful. Satisfied that he and his company have become solidly successful, and thankful that Roy's Rules have helped make it turn out that way.

Welcome to Solid Success!

Having heard our thoughts on Roy's Rules, are you now convinced that personal and company results that are anything less than *solidly successful* are absolutely unacceptable to you? Roy and I certainly hope so. We wish you well as you nourish your business and expand your life. America will be stronger for your efforts.

Appendix

A Summary of Roy's Rules

Guidelines for Solid Business Success *and* a Great Life

*ROY'S RULE NO. 1: **Be in Total Control... at the Helm***
No one can run your business like you can. You are the
entrepreneur who started it. You know where it can and
should be going. So take on the important tasks yourself.
Don't delegate to others the vital functions that produce
solid success. They belong in your personal care—all the
time! Don't give up the reins to anybody else. Stay at the
helm.

*ROY'S RULE NO. 2: **Get Into the Market***
Get out of your office! Get into the field! That's where you
belong much of the time. It's in the vital "externals" of the
business—markets, customers, business opportunities,
market and product positioning, suppliers and financing
sources—where you, and only you, can really find out
how to serve your customers best, seize profit opportunities, and make money.

ROY'S RULE NO. 3: Stay on Top of the Numbers

Owners make exceptional results happen by continually being on top of all the important numbers of their businesses, particularly the relationships that spell success, and the numbers that indicate real results. Relationships tell you how strong your company is financially. The key results numbers—working capital, costs, inventory and receivable turns, cash flow, gross margins and the like—tell you how you are going to make money. The important numbers have to be in your head at all times. They must be part of you, because they play a major role in every business decision you make.

ROY'S RULE NO. 4: Hammer Overhead

Allow only those overhead expenses that are absolutely required to get the job done—*and no more.* You only make money from direct labor. All other expenses are just so much excess baggage, and must be minimized or eliminated. This applies to all operating expenses, including management team and staff personnel. For maximum profits, fight nonproductive overhead costs every inch of the way. It's much easier to disallow a new expense than to get rid of an entrenched expense.

ROY'S RULE NO. 5: Simplify! Simplify! Simplify!

If you're going to own the most productive operation around, you simply must avoid unnecessary complexity. Running a highly successful, small, independent business is not all that tough if you keep everything simple. Complexity breeds costs—costs that cannot be permitted for maximum productivity, profitability and cash flow.

ROY'S RULE NO. 6: ***Go for Bona Fide Receivables***
Without solid, bona fide receivables, you're nothing! They are hard to find, especially in a down economy. But nothing is more important—and nothing will sink you faster than weak receivables. Select only great customers that produce bona fide receivables—receivables that are paid when you want them to be paid.

ROY'S RULE NO. 7: ***Think Cash***
If cash isn't flowing in the right direction for very long, you're company is history! Keeping sufficient cash in the till under all circumstances is vital to your liquidity, and therefore your business' longevity. That's fundamentally what business is all about—reaching a sound level of business where profitability and liquidity are continuous. Only the owner can act on all of the complex relationships that add up to positive cash flow.

ROY'S RULE NO. 8: ***Don't Lock In Assets***
It would be great to operate a profitable business without the need to fund any assets at all. Nice, but not practical! Most businesses need to employ assets to operate. But owners must make sure all assets are directly employed in *making money.* Assets that are locked into non-productive uses, such as fancy offices, slow-turning receivables or dead inventories, might as well be sitting on the moon.

ROY'S RULE NO. 9: ***Avoid Debt Like the Plague***
Create a discipline that leads to profits with longevity by financing longer-term capital requirements from internally generated funds. Relying on long-term debt or outside equity financing can quickly turn into a nightmare, raising costs and very possibly taking away your control over the future of your business.

ROY'S RULE NO. 10: *Keep Pushing Productivity and Quality*

Productivity and quality are never fixed quantities. They can always be improved, and they must be for your company to remain competitive. If you want to be a solidly successful force in your marketplace, you must search for operating practices and equipment that will increase the efficiency of your personnel and improve the quality and resulting value of your products and services. Keep pushing hard for continual improvements in productivity and quality.

ROY'S RULE NO. 11: *Be Very Wary of Growth*

Growth is a double-edged sword. It can get you where you want to be with your company, but it can also be a company-killer when "orderly" growth turns into a complete rout. It is absolutely not true that a company must grow, lest it die. Don't bite off more than you can chew. All of the owner's personal goals, including having a wonderful life, can be realized through solid, stable, right-sized operations where profits and cash flow can be maximized.

ROY'S RULE NO. 12: *Be Happy!*

Business is supposed to be fun. If it isn't, you're doing something wrong. If it is, you're making your company work for you, providing you with the time and resources you can devote to a complete and balanced family and personal life beyond the base business. Business owners who live balanced lives make better business owners.

About Herb Henderson

Co-author Herb Henderson is a management consultant specializing in results-improvement processes for independent business owners. His consulting firm, Focus Ltd., directs Great Ideas Exchanges, in which business owners exchange better operating ideas.

Herb's corporate background includes management positions with General Electric Company, Xerox Corp., and Schlumberger, Ltd. His fascination with the trials and opportunities of small-company ownership began when he founded and managed a regional distribution company prior to entering the consulting field.

Herb's educational background includes Harvard Business School (MBA) and Princeton University, from which he graduated with high honors, and was elected to Phi Beta Kappa. He lives on a ranch in Wyoming.

If you would like more information about managing an independent business for solid success, please call:

Focus Ltd.
(307) 455-2697